SO-EHH-466

THE
PROMOTIONAL
PLANNING
PROCESS

THE
PROMOTIONAL
PLANNING
PROCESS

 Roger A. Strang

PRAEGER

PRAEGER SPECIAL STUDIES • PRAEGER SCIENTIFIC

Published in 1980 by Praeger Publishers
CBS Educational and Professional Publishing
A Division of CBS, Inc.
521 Fifth Avenue, New York, New York 10017 U.S.A.

Library of Congress Catalog Card Number: 80-18848

0123456789 145 987654321

Printed in the United States of America

To my mother and the memory of my father

PREFACE

The subject of this book is the process by which promotional plans are developed and budgeted in large consumer goods manufacturing companies. In particular the book describes and models the decisions that are made, identifies the various executives involved in making these decisions, and assesses their roles. It also specifies the factors that influence the relative importance of advertising and sales promotion in brand-marketing strategy.

Recognition of the need for improved understanding of these subjects came in the course of a research project that I undertook for the Marketing Science Institute (MSI) of Cambridge, Massachusetts. This project involved an examination of the growth of sales promotion as an important element of marketing strategy and its likely impact on advertising and brand performance. During the course of the investigation, it became clear that a radical change had taken place in promotional strategy and that the prevailing view in the literature was outdated and misleading.

Most textbooks and articles that deal with the subject of promotional strategy appear to view advertising and personal selling as the two key elements. When they consider promotional planning, therefore, the principal strategic decision is the relative importance of each. However, for marketing executives in most consumer goods companies (and in an increasing number of companies in other areas), this is simply not the case. When promotional strategy is developed for individual products, personal selling is usually treated as a relatively fixed cost. Also, the personal-selling function itself is usually organized in a separate department, largely independent of the direct authority of the marketing manager. On the other hand, marketing executives are directly concerned with advertising and sales promotion activities, and, since most companies are now spending more on consumer and trade promotion than on advertising, the critical strategic issue is how the budget should be allocated between these two elements. This book examines and evaluates the way in which managers make this decision in the development of their promotional plans.

Most of the research on which this book is based was undertaken for my doctoral thesis at the Harvard Business School. In this regard I am deeply appreciative of the support given by the chairman of my doctoral committee, Professor Stephen Greyser. Under another of his "hats"—that of Executive Director of the MSI—he provided me with the opportunity to undertake this investigation and was unfalteringly encouraging as I wrestled with the problems of research in an essentially new field. The other members of my committee, Professors Robert Buzzell and Christine Urban, were also very helpful in forcing me to focus and clarify my ideas as the project developed.

The MSI was my home for two years, and I am grateful to the Managing Director, Alden Clayton, for his support and help with the data collection. Judy Kugel, Sherry Oliver, and Shannon Grady also provided cheerful assistance at many stages. It would have been impossible to undertake a study of this type without the support of many executives who freely gave large portions of their valuable time to provide the necessary data. I am deeply appreciative of their contribution. Several organizations were also helpful, including the 4A's Educational Foundation and the Association of National Advertisers.

This project was completed at the University of Southern California, and I am grateful for the assistance of the secretarial staff. I am also indebted to Judith Boyajian, who typed much of the manuscript and greatly eased the trials of authorship. Ron Brennan and Susan Badger of Praeger have also been particularly helpful in bringing the book to its final form.

CONTENTS

LIST OF TABLES AND FIGURES

THE
PROMOTIONAL
PLANNING
PROCESS

1
INTRODUCTION AND OVERVIEW

In recent years a growing number of executives, particularly in companies that market consumer goods and services, have become concerned about the dramatic changes that are taking place in the promotional strategies for their brands. This concern arises from their recognition that sales promotion activities have become an increasingly important part of their marketing effort. Sales promotion has traditionally been viewed as a minor supporting element in the total promotional program, but many companies now find themselves spending substantially more on sales promotion than on advertising. Although exact figures are difficult to obtain, it is generally accepted that total expenditures on sales promotion now exceed those for advertising and continue to grow at a faster rate.

Marketers are being forced to reappraise promotional strategies and are uncertain as to the correct course of action owing to the lack of understanding of the role of sales promotion, particularly in its relationship to advertising. These two elements are critical in the marketing strategy for many consumer goods and services. Change in their relative importance raises a number of questions: What is the relationship between advertising and sales promotion? Is this relationship recognized in planning promotional strategies? What factors influence the nature of the relationship—that is, cause managers to give greater weight to advertising or sales promotion in their marketing strategy? What mix of these elements is likely to be most effective for a particular product or service?

These questions are vital ones, but they have been virtually ignored in the marketing literature. Many of these issues are examined in this book, which presents the results of an extensive investigation of the process by which leading consumer goods companies develop advertising and sales promotion strategies. The

1

book is specifically concerned with the promotional planning process in large companies marketing consumer nondurable goods, the methods that companies use to allocate funds between advertising and sales promotion, and the internal, strategic, and environmental factors that influence those decisions.

DEFINITIONS

One of the basic problems in dealing with issues in <u>advertising</u> and <u>sales promotion strategy</u> lies in defining exactly what is meant by these two terms. The problem is particularly difficult in the case of <u>sales promotion</u> where there is a wide variety of definitions for the term. The American Marketing Association (AMA) Committee on Definitions (AMA 1960) has suggested these definitions:

<u>Advertising</u>—any paid form of nonpersonal presentation of ideas, goods, or services by an identifiable sponsor.

<u>Sales promotion</u>—those marketing activities, other than personal selling, advertising, and publicity, that stimulate consumer purchasing and dealer effectiveness, such as displays, shows and exhibitions, demonstrations, and various nonrecurrent selling efforts not in the ordinary routine.

These definitions provided by the AMA appear to be the most widely accepted and were the basis for those utilized in this book:

<u>Advertising</u>—all nonpersonal communication in measured media under identifiable sponsorship. This includes television, radio, outdoor, transit, and print media. Advertisements for sales promotion programs (for example, a print advertisement that primarily advertises a premium offer or a price reduction) are excluded when possible. Production costs of advertising are usually included in company data and excluded when possible. Production costs of advertising are usually incorporated in company data and deleted from the information prepared by organizations that provide estimates of company-advertising expenditures.

<u>Sales promotion</u>—all other forms of sponsored communications apart from activities traditionally associated with personal selling. Sales promotion thus includes trade shows and exhibits, couponing (manufacturer and retail), sampling, premiums, trade allowances, contests, cents-off packs, refund offers, free goods, bonus packs, point-of-purchase materials, sales literature, consumer education, and demonstration activities.

The definitions used in this book are rather more specific than those of the AMA. This was done deliberately to facilitate the analysis of quantitative data relating to advertising and sales promotion expenditures both within a company and from the trade press.

OVERVIEW OF THE STUDY

The issue of the relationship between advertising and sales promotion and the development of appropriate promotional strategies is obviously large and complex. It is also an important issue, made even more pertinent by the dramatic changes in the promotional mix that have taken place in recent years. However, a review of the literature shows that very little attention has been paid to the basic process by which advertising/sales promotion strategy is developed, let alone to the evaluation of the effectiveness of different strategies.

Therefore, this investigation was designed to provide basic information about promotional strategy by focusing on the process by which the strategic decisions are made. The overall objective was to determine the process by which advertising and sales promotion strategy was developed, funded, and implemented for established brands of consumer nondurable goods. Within this framework specific attention was given to the promotional planning process, the decision models used to allocate funds between advertising and sales promotion, the organizational factors that influence promotional plans, the impact of marketing strategy on promotional plans, and the environmental factors that influence promotional strategy decisions.

The study was carried out in two phases. The first involved personal interviews with executives in a variety of functions and at different levels in a number of consumer goods manufacturing companies as well as advertising and sales promotion agencies. The findings of this phase were used to develop a questionnaire instrument that was used to survey senior marketing executives in large companies that manufacture consumer nondurable goods. This provided a larger information base relating to the promotional planning process and the factors that influenced the allocation of funds.

The findings of the study include a detailed description of the planning process and the specification of a number of different methods that respondents used to allocate their total budget between advertising and sales promotion. The various participants in the promotional planning process are identified and their roles described, with particular attention to the changing position of the product manager and the emerging role of the sales promotion specialist. A comprehensive list of other factors that influence the allocation decision was compiled and the direction of their influence evaluated. On the basis of these findings, various implications are drawn relating to obstacles to effective decision making and the development of successful promotional strategies. Some implications for the academic community are assessed and areas for future inquiry suggested.

This book is essentially descriptive in nature in an effort to provide basic information about a complex and changing area of decision making that has received little research attention. The conclusions are also restricted in their focus on the larger manufacturers of consumer nondurable goods and, therefore, cannot be generalized for all companies. However, information is drawn from more than 70 companies to ensure the maximum diversity of product types, organizational structures, planning procedures, and company size. The detailed presentation of the findings attempts to capture this diversity by presenting alternate practices as well as commonly observed patterns of behaviors.

The remainder of this chapter provides additional background material on the changes in promotional strategy and highlights the importance of this issue for companies in many different industries. Chapter 2 describes the methodology used in the investigation in greater detail, while Chapter 3 explores the findings as they relate to the promotional planning process. Several models of the allocation decision are presented in Chapter 4. Chapters 5, 6, and 7 examine the impacts of the organization, the marketing strategies selected, and the environment, respectively, on promotional strategy. The final chapter, Chapter 8, summarizes the findings of the research and discusses their implications.

MAJOR ISSUES IN STRATEGY DEVELOPMENT

The research on which this book is based was primarily concerned with improving our understanding of one element of marketing strategy. Marketing strategy has been defined as "the set of objectives, policies and rules that guides over time the firm's marketing efforts—its level, mix and allocation—partly independently and partly in response to changing environmental conditions" (Kotler 1972, p. 46). Issues in marketing strategy may therefore arise in three areas: the development of the objectives, policies, and rules; the translation of these into plans and budgets specifying the level and mix of effort and the allocation of resources; and the independent and environmental factors that affect decisions in this area.

Just as marketing strategy itself is one element of overall corporate strategy, so marketing strategy is made up of a number of substrategies. These are typically classified into four groups: product, price, distribution, and promotion. Advertising and sales promotion, together with personal selling and publicity, are the major elements of the promotional substrategy. Management's task is "making sure that the elements of a marketing strategy add up to an integrated and interrelated totality" (Buzzell et al., 1972, p. 329). This means that each substrategy has to be integrated and interrelated and that the determination of these will involve the same issues as for the overall marketing strategy.

Issues in advertising and sales promotion strategy, therefore, arise in the same areas as for marketing strategy in general, namely: the objectives, policies, and rules that guide advertising and sales promotion strategy; the amount that is budgeted for advertising and sales promotion activities and the process by which it is allocated to each of them; and the independent and environmental factors that affect these decisions.

IMPORTANCE OF ADVERTISING AND SALES
PROMOTION IN MARKETING STRATEGY

The specific issue of the relationship among the elements of promotional strategy is important to senior management. Robinson and Luck (1964) found that "of all the decisions marketing managers must take, questions concerning promotional allocations are thought to be the most difficult and troublesome" (p. 3). Buzzell et al. (1972) agree, saying that "establishing the total level of communications effort and its allocation among major forms are difficult but vital management tasks" (p. 539).

The allocation between advertising and sales promotion is of particular importance not only because of the amount of money involved—an estimated $50 billion was expected to be spent on advertising and sales promotion in 1975 (Bowman 1974)—but also because for many companies these may be the two most highly leveraged elements in marketing strategy. This is shown in the results of a survey by Udell (1968), who asked senior marketing executives to allocate 100 points among all the elements of marketing strategy according to their perceived importance. Advertising and sales promotion together were allocated an average of 52 points by executives marketing consumer durable goods and 62 points by executives in nondurable goods companies. In product categories such as cosmetics and toiletries, total expenditures on advertising and sales promotion may be more than 50 percent of sales receipts for certain brands.

Advertising and sales promotion are also leveraged in that they may be the most easily manipulated elements of the marketing mix. Most large companies use the product manager system, and in most of these companies a major responsibility of these executives is the preparation of an annual marketing plan and budget for their products. In theory the product or brand manager has considerable freedom to choose from many strategic options, including price changes and changes in packaging, product quality, distribution, or expenditures on marketing research. However, in practice, especially in companies marketing consumer nondurable goods, "the greatest latitude in planning lies in the contribution margin," because, after meeting the target return, "this represents so many dollars which he can divide between advertising and sales promotion" (Kotler 1972, p. 395).

The importance of advertising and sales promotion in marketing strategy for consumer goods is supported by Hopkins (1972). In his study he found that company marketing plans usually emphasized the key sales-generating elements and that plans of consumer-product manufacturers "usually focus more on the advertising and sales promotion elements" (p. 6). Ames (1968) also noted that in a consumer goods company "advertising, promotion and merchandising are generally the core elements of the marketing plan" (p. 102).

CHANGES IN THE RELATIONSHIP
BETWEEN ADVERTISING AND SALES PROMOTION

The question of the most appropriate allocation of funds is particularly pertinent at the present time because of recent major changes in the relative importance of advertising and sales promotion in marketing strategy. Expenditures on sales promotion have been growing much faster than advertising outlays in recent years and are now estimated to be significantly higher.

An analysis of Advertising Age data (Bowman 1974) suggested that sales promotion expenditures increased at an average rate of 9.5 percent per annum between 1969 and 1974. This growth rate was almost twice that of advertising. In 1975 it was estimated that total sales promotion expenditures would be 40 percent greater than those for advertising. This is a complete reversal of the conclusions of a 1958 study that estimated total advertising expenditures to be four times those for sales promotion (Spratlen 1962).

In certain categories, particularly consumer nondurable goods, the increase in the relative importance of sales promotion has been even more marked. A 1956 study found that sales promotion accounted for less than 10 percent of the advertising and sales promotion budget for companies marketing toiletries and only 24 percent for companies marketing packaged goods. In comparison a 1977 survey of packaged-goods companies found that the sales promotion allocation had risen to an average of 58 percent.

The growth of sales promotion is not confined to consumer non-durables. Manufacturers of durables are also increasing their use of sales promotion. For example, in 1975 General Electric joined with other appliance manufacturers in offering rebates and continued and expanded this program through 1977. The automobile companies were also heavy users of rebates in early 1975. The change has also involved service industries, including banks, insurance companies, fast-food restaurants, and the airlines.

The underlying causes for this growth have been discussed in an earlier study (Strang 1975). They include an increased willingness by senior management to accept sales promotion techniques as "legitimate," the appointment of sales promotion specialists to aid planning, and the expanded use of the product manager system with its pressure for short-term results. The most important contributing factors are changes in the marketplace (including higher levels of competitive activity), a slowdown in market growth during the 1973-75 recession, rapidly escalating media costs, and increasing pressure for larger and more sophisticated retail chains in the food, drug, and general merchandise areas.

In light of these reasons, it appears that the change in the promotional mix is not temporary and that sales promotion is likely to be the major element in the foreseeable future. It is the dominant role of sales promotion that has caused considerable concern to marketing executives. Although the empirical evidence is limited, there is a widespread belief that too great a reliance on sales promotion—at the expense of advertising—can harm both an individual brand and a product category. The basis for this belief is the perception that, since sales promotions are essentially additional incentives to purchase, the constant use of these devices will damage the quality image of the product or service, encourage increased brand switching, and possibly lower consumption. A vice-president of marketing at the American Can Company reflected this view when he concluded that "sales promotion is the added reason to buy. . . . When the added reason to buy drowns out the basic reason to buy to this extent, branded goods selling is in serious trouble" (Weber 1973). Comments such as this reinforce the need for research in this area to aid in the development of effective promotional strategies.

2
OBJECTIVES AND METHODOLOGY

OBJECTIVES

The first step toward improving promotional strategy in decision making must be to gather basic information on the way those decisions are made. As Bauer (1972) has noted, "We want to understand organizational processes in order to improve them." A review
of the literature found only one previous study of advertising and
sales promotion strategy; this study focused on new brands and was
undertaken in 1963 before sales promotion assumed its present importance. Therefore, it was decided that the overall objective should
be, as noted earlier, to determine the process by which advertising
and sales promotion strategy is developed, funded, and implemented
for established brands of consumer nondurable goods.

In the preceding chapter it was concluded that issues in promotional strategy would arise in three areas: the development of objectives and policies, the translation of these into plans and budgets, and
the examination of independent and environmental factors that would
influence the decision. On this basis the specific objectives for the
study were defined as follows:

1. To describe the process by which funds are budgeted for
advertising and sales promotion activities for established brands of
consumer nondurable goods. This process would include both the
development of objectives and policies and their translation into plans
and budgets. In this context an issue of particular interest would be
the decision models used by executives to allocate funds between advertising and sales promotion.

2. To identify and evaluate the impact of factors within the organization that influences promotional strategy. The earlier study of

promotional planning had strongly emphasized the importance of "organizational attributes" in the development of promotional strategy. These include the position of the decision maker(s), their freedom to make decisions, and the degree of coordination between information and planning. The overall marketing strategy decided upon by the organization would also be a major determinant of the promotional strategy.

3. To identify and evaluate the impact of factors in the external environment that influences promotional strategy. The importance of environmental factors was noted earlier. These are likely to include the stage in the product life cycle as well as the various market, competitive, consumer, and distributional conditions.

There are two main reasons for focusing on the decision process for established brands. First, the process for new brands has been extensively studied (Robinson and Luck 1964), while virtually no attention has been paid to the decision process for established brands. In fact Hopkins (1972) found that the differences in the marketing planning process for new and established brands were so great that they were usually undertaken independently. The second reason is, simply, that established brands are much more numerous on the market, so managers make many more decisions about them than about new brands. It also appears that the major shifts in advertising/sales promotion strategy involve the established brands.

A similar rationale underlies the decision to restrict the focus to consumer nondurable goods. Although, as noted earlier, there have been increases in the relative importance of sales promotion in consumer durables and services, it is among consumer nondurables that the change has been greatest. These companies are also the largest users of advertising—60 of the 100 largest advertisers in 1975, according to Advertising Age ("Advertising" 1976)—and are likely to have the largest expenditures on sales promotion. Therefore, these companies are likely to employ the most sophisticated planning and budgeting procedures—to be the leaders in the field. Research oriented around these companies will not only significantly benefit the major users of advertising and sales promotion but will also be of value to companies in other areas where planning and budgeting procedures are less advanced. Many studies of promotional decision making have adopted this focus, including Robinson and Luck (1964), Lucas (1972), Courtney (1970), Buell (1973), and San Augustine and Foley (1975).

A further justification is that executives in consumer nondurable goods companies have expressed the most concern for the changing advertising/sales promotion mix and are therefore the most likely to use the findings. It is recognized that this is a limitation in that it will not be possible to compare allocation decisions for different types of goods (although Robinson and Luck [1964] found many similarities between the promotional planning process for consumer goods and industrial goods).

METHODOLOGY

Phase 1—Personal Interviews

Because of the paucity of research in the area of advertising/sales promotion decision making, it was decided to undertake the study in two phases. The first phase would involve a series of exploratory personal interviews with executives in a limited number of different companies. The development of strategy is a complex process, and so personal interviews were felt to be essential. The second phase would build on the findings of these interviews in a broader survey of a larger number of companies conducted through a mail questionnaire.

The objectives of the personal interview phase were to describe the process (or processes) by which funds were budgeted for advertising and sales promotion, identify the members of the organization who were involved in this decision process and determine their roles, and prepare an extensive list of factors that influence the allocation of funds to advertising and sales promotion and describe the direction of this influence.

The companies in which interviews were to be conducted were selected from among the larger manufacturers of consumer nondurable goods, because these were perceived as employing the most sophisticated planning procedures and as most likely to give the greatest care to the preparation of advertising and sales promotion programs. The information gathered in these interviews would not, then, be representative of all advertisers, but, as Buell (1973) noted in his similarly focused study of advertising decision making, it will be "significant in reflecting what the leading companies and advertisers are doing" (p. viii).

The criteria for selection were: companies with a leadership position in the field; companies that represented a cross section of product categories within the consumer nondurable goods field, including the major areas of food, household products, and personal-care products; companies that spent a significant amount on advertising and sales promotion; and companies that were willing to participate. The author decided to seek interviews with approximately ten companies, with the cutoff point being when duplication of responses indicated that most important factors had been identified.

TABLE 2.1

Personal Interviews: Companies by Product Category

Category	Number
Primarily food products	4
Primarily personal-care products	4
Primarily household products	3
Other products	2
Advertising and sales promotion agencies	5
Total	18

In addition to the manufacturers, the author opted to seek interviews with advertising and sales promotion agencies. These agencies are involved in the planning and budgeting process, and so they would provide an additional perspective. Since they have many clients, executives might be expected to have a broader range of experience with companies (including smaller manufacturers and service organizations) that were not included in the study. In the end, executives from 13 companies and 5 outside agencies were interviewed. These provided a broad coverage of the major categories of consumer goods as can be seen in Table 2.1.

The companies interviewed were all among the leaders in their fields. All were among the 100 leading advertisers of 1975 as identified by Advertising Age. Annual sales totals ranged from $100 million to several billion. The advertising agencies included 3 of the top 20 in annual billings.

Within each company interviews were sought with a variety of executives in different functions and at different levels. This approach has been adopted by a number of researchers as the best method of establishing the process by which strategic decisions are made in an organization. In most cases a number of executives are involved at different stages of the decision process, and so no one executive may be fully aware of all the factors that influence the outcome. In addition, executives tend to view the process subjectively, and this may bias their views of their roles. A vertical and horizontal cross section of respondents within one division or company allows a check on the decision process and the roles of the various participants.

TABLE 2.2

Personal Interviews: Executives by Area of Responsibility

Area	Number
General management	4
Marketing/product management	19
Research and planning	19
Sales promotion	13
Advertising	7
Sales management	3
Finance	2
Total	67

Interviews were sought with corporate and division managers, marketing and product managers, and managers of advertising, sales promotion, and sales, as well as executives in market research, planning, and finance. Table 2.2 shows that a broad range of functional areas was represented in the interviews. A wide variety of levels of responsibility were also covered in the interviews. Respondents ranged from division general managers and corporate vice-presidents through various levels of management to senior staff executives. An analysis of respondents by level of responsibility is shown in Table 2.3.

Since this was a preliminary inquiry, interviews were largely unstructured. However, in order to ensure that all topics were covered and to assist respondents, an interview guide was prepared and made available as requested. A copy is presented in Appendix B. The guide was essentially a list of topic headings and was designed to encourage a broad range of responses.

In order to bring general comments into sharper focus, respondents were asked later in the interview to discuss the budgeting process for a specific brand. In a further step to ensure that as many influencing factors as possible would be identified, some respondents were asked to consider two or more brands within their division or company. These brands were selected on the basis of either having different ratios of advertising expenditures to total advertising and sales promotion or being in different stages of their life cycles.

TABLE 2.3

Personal Interviews: Respondents by Rank

Rank	Number
Division president/executive vice-president/ general manager	4
Corporate vice-president	7
Department heads	15
Marketing managers/group product managers	8
Product/brand managers	9
Other directors and managers	13
Other executives	11
Total	67

The first criterion was selected on the basis that there was insufficient research to justify a priori assumptions as to the factors that influenced advertising/sales promotion budgeting. The second criterion was a deliberate attempt to seek evidence to support the theory that different advertising/sales promotion expenditure patterns are common at different stages of the brand life cycle.

Both these concepts were well understood by most respondents, although some had to calculate the advertising/sales promotion ratio since it was not always provided in their budget analysis. It was found that these approaches overlapped considerably. Brands with a high ratio of advertising to sales promotion were generally in the growth or early-maturity stage of their life cycle, while brands where sales promotion was more important than advertising were in the late-maturity or decline stage.

Interviews generally lasted from one-half hour to two and one-half hours, with most being about one hour in duration. Several respondents were reinterviewed, both in person and by telephone. Respondents also made available written material, including memorandums, plans, budgets, policy statements, and reports, which were used to support the analysis.

Phase 2—Mail Survey

The second phase of the study was a mail survey of executives in consumer goods manufacturing companies. The use of a mail sur-

vey to study issues such as this is relatively common, since it is the
only practical way to secure this type of information from executives
in a large number of companies. In this instance it provided a basis
for exploring the extent to which the findings of the interview study
applied to other organizations.

The specific objectives of this phase of the study were to determine the applicability of the advertising/sales promotion budgeting
process described in the first phase of the study, compare different
organizational structures and roles as they related to this decision
process, and assess among executives in a large number of companies
the perceived impact of internal and external factors previously identified as influencing the advertising/sales promotion budget decision.

The samples of companies to be surveyed was drawn from two
sources. The first of these was the Advertising Age list of the 60
largest advertisers in 1975 that manufactured consumer nondurable
goods. The second source consisted of the company representatives
of members of the Association of National Advertisers (ANA). The
sample was therefore heavily weighted toward large manufacturers
of consumer nondurable goods. The advantages and disadvantages of
this weighting have already been discussed.

The senior marketing executive in each division or major product group within the Advertising Age companies was selected as the
primary respondent. The reasons for this included the greater experience and broader perspective of executives in these positions.
The preliminary interviews showed that they were fully involved in
the planning process for individual brands yet at a level high enough
so that they could interact with managers in other functional areas
and with corporate-level executives (to avoid overlaps, no corporate
executives were included). These executives, as well as the ANA
representative in the other companies, could also be personally identified and addressed—a factor that was expected to increase the response rate.

The questionnaire was highly structured to make it as easy as
possible for respondents to answer and thus to maximize the response
rate. The extensive preliminary interviews that took place provided
sufficient information to cover most alternatives. Nevertheless,
space was provided for additional responses throughout the questionnaire, and a large section at the end asked for any further comments
or opinions on questions that were not raised. A copy of the questionnaire is included in Appendix A.

Other steps were taken to encourage respondents to complete
the necessarily lengthy questionnaire. The questionnaire was printed
both to indicate the importance of the study and to guide respondents
easily through the eight pages by use of different type sizes and faces.
A cover letter mentioned the critical and current nature of the subject

together with an indication of the lack of relevant information known about the area. Reference was made to previous research conducted by the author and the high level of interest that had been shown by the business community. Respondents were offered copies of the final report from this study and of an earlier article on sales promotion management.

In order to improve the accuracy of the responses, questions were focused on concrete actions. As already mentioned, the decision-making process is largely intangible, and the full complexities can never be captured in a questionnaire. However, as far as possible identifiable steps in the process were used—for example, establish sales targets, prepare brand-advertising program, and approve advertising budget. The roles of individuals were also differentiated as specifically as possible—for example, not involved/consulted/prepares proposals or buidelines/approves. Of course, there was the possibility of varied interpretations, but cross-check questions were included.

The questionnaire was organized into four sections of related questions to aid respondents in developing their answers:

Part 1. This part focused on organizational structure and responsibilities. These questions were relatively straightforward and factual to encourage the respondent to begin completing the questionnaire.

Part 2. The second section was the core of the study and addressed the more complex issues relating to the advertising and sales promotion planning and budgeting process. A final extensive question in this section asked respondents to assess the impact, if any, of various internal and external factors that had been found from the personal interviews.

Part 3. This section was a short one asking respondents to describe their advertising and sales promotion research and evaluation procedures.

Part 4. The final section asked respondents to provide information about their division and corporation to aid in classifying responses.

The questionnaire was extensively tested and revised over a period of several months both in-house and in the field.

The Advertising Age list provided 241 names, and there were 255 on the list provided by the ANA, for a total distribution of 496. By the final due date a total of 64 questionnaires had been returned for a response rate of 13 percent. Of these 64, 7 responses were deleted, either because they were not from manufacturers of consumer nondurable goods or because the possibility existed of overlap with another response from the same company. The screening procedure that was used to check against duplicate responses (that is, two from the same division or from a corporate and division executive in the same company) is described in Appendix C.

Although the response rate is the same as Banks (1973) reported for his similar study with the same group of respondents, it is not as high as was expected. There are a number of possible reasons for this, including the length and complexity of the questionnaire (despite efforts to make it easy for respondents to complete) and the fact that the ANA listing incorporated a substantial number of companies that saw themselves as being in businesses other than consumer nondurable goods and, therefore, rejected the questionnaire. There were also problems in the distribution of the questionnaire. The first mailing was delayed and was further slowed by early Christmas mail, while the follow-up mailing arrived at a time when a number of businesses in the Northeast and Midwest were closed or experiencing setbacks with the worst winter in many years.

The response rate is somewhat misleading, however, in terms of the range of companies represented. Most respondents included their name and address, and it appeared, as Banks (1973) had also found, that the majority of companies delegated one person to reply on behalf of the whole organization, rather than completing a separate questionnaire for each division. This meant that the 57 responses provided information on planning practices in an estimated 55 different companies. At least 25 of these companies were from the Advertising Age list so that almost one-half of the 60 largest advertisers of consumer nondurable goods were included.

An analysis of the respondents, in fact, indicates that many of the survey objectives were obtained in the sample of responses.

TABLE 2.4

Mail Survey: Companies by Product Category

Category	Number
Dry groceries	18
Perishables	4
Personal care/toiletries	16
Household nonfood	19
Total	57

TABLE 2.5

Mail Survey: Companies by Size

Sales (millions of dollars)	Number
Division sales	
Less than 25	3
25 to 49	6
50 to 99	9
100 or more	39
Total	57
Corporate sales	
Less than 100	1
100 to 499	10
More than 500	39
Not applicable	7
Total	57

TABLE 2.6

Mail Survey: Companies by Organizational Structure

Structure	Number
Single corporate entity	7
Divisionalized company with marketing at corporate and division level	11
Divisionalized company with marketing at division level only	39
Total	57

17

TABLE 2.7

Mail Survey: Respondents by Position

Position	Number
Marketing management	22
Marketing services	10
Advertising or sales promotion specialist	15
General management	6
Not specified	4
Total	57

Table 2.4 shows that the three main categories of consumer nondurable goods products—namely, food, personal care, and household nonfoods—were well represented. Table 2.5 indicates that, although the bulk of respondents represented larger divisions and companies, 32 percent reported division sales of less than $100 million. There were seven respondents from companies that did not have a divisionalized organizational structure (see Table 2.6). In regard to the respondents themselves, the objectives of securing responses from senior executives was clearly achieved. There were only two respondents who identified themselves as product managers, with the majority giving their title as "manager," "director," or "vice-president" (see Table 2.7).

Thus it cannot be said that this sample of respondents is truly representative of all manufacturers of consumer nondurable goods. However, the sample does include a substantial number of the larger manufacturers as well as a diverse range of product categories and organizational structures. The responses of this sample are therefore likely to provide useful insights into the promotional decision-making practices of large manufacturers of consumer nondurable goods.

METHODOLOGICAL LIMITATIONS

A study of this nature has a number of methodological limitations arising in both the interview phase and the mail survey. Although the interviews were conducted among a larger number of companies than in earlier studies in this area, the number was still limited and, as has been noted, heavily weighted to large, successful companies and agencies. Within the companies themselves there was the possibility of bias since management selected the products that were to be the focus of the study and had a strong influence on the individuals who were to be interviewed.

There are also limitations due to the interview method itself. Although a diverse range of executives was interviewed, they were asked about past events, and important aspects could have been forgotten or glossed over in a desire to present the planning process and/or the individual's role in the best possible light. There is also the possibility of bias by the interviewer, which could have influenced the information sought as well as its recording and analysis. While these are potentially major limitations, many of the conclusions drawn from the preliminary interviews have been tested in presentation to a wider group of executives and have been well accepted as accurate representation of practices in many companies.

The mail survey was subject to a similar limitation because, although the sample was considerably larger and more diverse, it was still heavily weighted to larger companies. In addition, the questionnaire may be viewed as a source of bias. Although based on extensive interviews, it is highly structured and therefore limited in the diversity of behavior that can be captured. Great care was taken in formulating and testing the questions themselves, but misinterpretations are always possible, especially in an essentially qualitative subject area. There are also potential problems in asking one person to report on the typical planning process for all brands in one division or company since practices may vary.

In no sense, then, can the findings of this research be said to be statistically representative of all companies or even of all consumer nondurable goods manufacturers. This does not mean that the findings are not significant. The interviews and the survey together with the case studies that were reviewed led to the incorporation of views of more than 70 different consumer nondurable goods manufacturers. Most of these companies are large, and they include more than half of the 60 largest advertisers who market consumer nondurable goods. A considerable variety of viewpoints has been incorporated through the involvement of smaller companies, companies that do not employ the product manager system. They represent all product types within the consumer nondurable goods area. The findings, therefore, are, in Buell's (1973) words, "significant in reflecting what the leading companies in the field are doing."

3
PROMOTIONAL PLANNING AND
THE APACS MODEL

To understand how advertising and sales promotion strategy is developed, it is important to examine the process within which promotional plans are determined and implemented. In this regard there have been many studies of the advertising planning and budgeting process (see, for example, Buell 1973; Hurwood 1968; Marschner 1967; Permut 1977; San Augustin and Foley 1975). These studies have adopted a variety of perspectives, including industrial goods as well as consumer products and both the creative planning activity and the allocation of advertising funds to geographic areas. However, there has been virtually no attention given to the sales promotion planning and budgeting process. Christopher (1972a) undertook a study of sales promotion planning in the United Kingdom, but in this country the subject has been only indirectly considered in conjunction with studies on the effects of different types of sales promotion.

The planning and budgeting process for both advertising and sales promotion has received even less attention, for, despite the growing recognition of their close relationship, a review of the literature revealed only one study that specifically considered the process for both these elements. This work was undertaken by Robinson and Luck (1964) and was "devoted to the problem of how funds for the promotional mix of advertising, personal selling and sales promotion were allocated" (p. 3). Their study was restricted to new products and they investigated the planning process for one such product in each of six consumer goods companies and six industrial goods companies.

Through interviews with company executives and an examination of reports and memorandums, they found that, while each company had its own approach to decision making, there were sufficient similarities to develop a "reference structure (or conceptual model) of the decision making process" (p. 4). They called this reference

FIGURE 3.1

Adaptive Planning and Control Sequence (APACS)

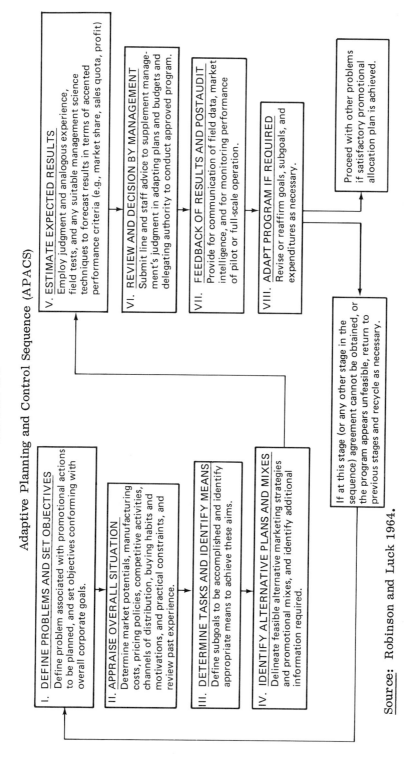

Source: Robinson and Luck 1964.

21

structure the Adaptive Planning and Control Sequence (APACS), and it divided the decision process into eight steps as outlined in Figure 3.1.

Following the decision to introduce a new product, the first stage involves setting objectives for the promotional program and establishing a total budget. This is followed by an extensive review of the market and competitive situation, which leads to the determination of subgoals to guide the allocation of effort and to the identification of appropriate promotional techniques. Alternative marketing and promotional strategies are then considered and tested by comparing their expected outcomes. The plan is then presented to higher management for their approval and implemented. There are regular reviews of the plan, and there may be modifications of the promotional program if results differ from those expected.

Robinson and Luck note that this schema

> reflects a variety of experiences as to how promotional allocation decisions may be described in sequence. In practice, not every one of the eight steps depicted receives equal emphasis, nor are they executed explicitly or systematically. Nevertheless, at least implicitly, all these steps occur. [P. 34]

Although this framework was developed on the basis of a study of promotional allocation decisions for new products, it appears to be broadly applicable to other promotional decisions. It is therefore used as a basis for analyzing the allocation process for the established brands in this study. The bulk of this chapter is thus concerned with examining each of the APACS stages in order to compare the findings of the present research with those of Robinson and Luck and to determine the applicability of the APACS model to the decision process for established brands.

APPLICABILITY OF THE APACS MODEL

Define Problem and Set Objectives

The first step in the APACS model of the promotional planning process involved defining the problem with which marketing activities would be concerned and setting objectives conforming with overall corporate goals. This included some review of the market situation for the brand and the establishment of sales targets, financial goals, and total budget.

During the interviews it became apparent that in one sense this could be described as a more important stage for established brands

than for the new brands studied by Robinson and Luck. The reason
for this is the greater amount of information that is available concerning the brand and its markets. Thus, a more detailed review of the
market situation can be attempted and broad trends more clearly assessed. In several cases it was found that this review was undertaken
in conjunction with an update of the long-term plan for the brand.
These plans typically covered a period of three or five years and as
a minimum included sales and profit projections. In at least one company, the long-term plan also incorporated a general statement of objectives and strategy and a broad breakdown of expected expenses, including the proportions to be allocated to advertising and sales promotion.

In all the companies that were interviewed, it appeared that the
amount of planning activity at this stage was closely related to the
brand's performance. If sales and profits were as expected, then the
review followed the formal procedures laid down and there was little
discussion. If the brand was failing to meet expectations (or in one
case was substantially exceeding them), then the review was undertaken in more detail, more long-term projections were prepared, and
substantial discussion took place to determine the appropriate goals
and budgets.

Although specific promotional objectives were rarely established
at this stage, the promotional program was strongly influenced by the
decisions that were made. The first of these was the decision on a
sales target, which then became the objective that the promotional
activities would be expected to achieve. It is true that this goal would
be sought in conjunction with other elements of the marketing mix,
but, as noted earlier, for many consumer nondurable goods, promotional activities are likely to be most important strategic elements.

The second decision involved the setting of financial goals for
the brand. This determines the amount that will be available for promotional activities since, as Robinson and Luck found, the total promotional budget was invariably calculated as a residual from sales
after providing for other costs and the desired profit.

In two of the companies that were studied, the impact was even
greater, as the actual allocation for advertising and sales promotion
was specified at this stage. Both of these were companies that had
adopted a policy of classifying brands into strategic groups for different strategic treatments. The effect of this approach on promotional strategy will be discussed in greater detail in Chapter 4.

In fact, this stage in the planning process for established brands
might be better termed target planning and divided into several sub-
stages including situational analysis, establishment of targets and
budgets, and approval. Among the companies in the interview study,
the most common approach to this phase appeared to be that the product manager and the research staff would review the situation and set

objectives and budgets that were then approved and/or revised by senior management up to the corporate level. The alternate procedure was for the corporate planning department to prepare its own forecasts and for the corporation to recommend targets to the division management. In one company both procedures were used. Regardless of the specific approach, this stage marked a major degree of involvement by corporate management, which was not generally seen again until much later in the decision process.

This level of senior management involvement is confirmed by the results of a survey shown in Table 3.1. For a majority of the respondents, the brand financial goals are established by executives above the product manager level. In almost one-third of the cases, senior marketing, division and corporation executives also have responsibility for setting and sales goals and establishing the preliminary marketing budget. The product manager is the most likely to have responsibility for all but one of these activities. The relationships between the product manager and other executives is discussed in Chapter 5.

Appraise Overall Situation

All planners in the interview phase were found to make an extensive review of the environment, and, unlike those interviewed by Robinson and Luck, all collected information on most of the areas suggested by the model. Differences among the planners appeared to result from the extent to which they utilized information from special studies. One company employed a monitoring study of consumer awareness, attitudes, and buying habits for its major products, which was fielded every six months. Another company used consumer panel data on a continuing basis. In both cases the planners had more up-to-date information on consumers than their colleagues in other companies who may have only had information from a "one-shot" study or indirectly via audit data and sales reports.

In a similar manner, the planners interviewed appeared more likely to draw specific conclusions from their appraisals than those questioned by Robinson and Luck. They found only one planner who explicitly recorded conclusions, but most planners in this study were required to present their analyses and conclusions in the written planning document. This supports Hopkins's (1972) survey of marketing planning in which he found that most companies required written plans and that these included an evaluation of the environment and conclusions as to the problems and opportunities for the brand.

The product manager's responsibility for this situational analysis was confirmed by the survey as shown in Table 3.1. The few cases where the product manager does not have responsibility could reflect companies that do not use the product manager system.

Determine Tasks and Identify Means

During the interview phase, it was found that one outcome of the extensive situational analysis was often a more detailed sales forecast that incorporated more recent information on the current year's performance. However, the emphasis was generally on predicting sales by periods in the coming year rather than on changing the original forecast and budget. Unless there was a major change in the market situation, respondents reported that the original forecast and budget figures would be retained and incorporated into the final plan.

This forecast was used as a guide in the next stage of the promotional planning process, which involved defining "subgoals for the allocation of effort" and the identification of "appropriate tools . . . to accomplish the tasks required" (Robinson and Luck 1964, p. 36). In regard to the definition of objectives for specific promotional activities, most planners who were interviewed were required to put these in writing as part of the formal planning document. This was especially true for advertising goals, which were set in virtually every case.

Robinson and Luck found that only one-third of their planners wrote down these objectives and that in all but one case these objectives were put in writing only after the promotional plan had been prepared. This appeared to be the procedure for several firms in this present study, but a number of instances of formal commitment to objectives were also found. These examples were characteristic of companies where the planners were required to obtain approval of objectives from their superiors before proceeding with further planning.

Whether they were written before or after the plan was prepared, the fact that they were written did not guarantee that all objectives were of equal value in guiding the allocation effort. In fact, there appeared to be two major weaknesses in the objectives set by companies in the interview study. The first was the failure—in several instances —to define objectives in measurable terms. Thus, one objective for a brand was "To increase sales to current users," with no indication as to the amount of increase that was expected.

The second area of weakness was a failure to relate objectives to particular promotional activities. When questioned, most planners perceived differences in the roles of advertising and sales promotion, although often these overlapped. One planner, for example, saw advertising as being good for securing trial of the brand, while sales promotion gained both trial and repurchase. However, this understanding was not often found in the written plan, where one set of promotional objectives was established with no indication of the roles of advertising or sales promotion.

An example of this latter problem is provided in the reported strategy for L'eggs pantyhose (Singer and DeBruicker 1975b). Here the "advertising and promotion objectives" were to:

a) build strong brand awareness and recognition of our logo and package;
b) let the consumer know where L'eggs was available, that it was new and different, and that it would become a permanent grocery and drugstore feature;
c) stress our major product attribute, that L'eggs fit better than any other hosiery product;
d) show the display and package in all advertising to make them synonymous with the L'eggs program. [P. 4]

In this case there was apparently no indication as to the relative roles of advertising or sales promotion in achieving these objectives.

As can be seen from Table 3.1, the mail survey showed that the product manager was principally responsible for establishing the objectives for both advertising and sales promotion. As with the situational analysis, the other responses probably are from companies that did not use the product manager system. These results do not reflect the fact that—as observed in the interviews—objectives were often set after discussions with several groups, including the functional specialists, senior management, and the advertising agency.

Identify Alternative Plans and Mixes

One of the major differences between the APACS model and the planning process for established brands was observed at stage four. The model suggests that at this stage companies identify and evaluate alternative plans and mixes, but little of this was found among the companies that were studied in the interview phase. Robinson and Luck reported that alternative allocations to advertising and sales promotion were considered in 5 of their 12 cases. However, although there was a limited amount of informal consideration, only one of the companies in this investigation required that planners prepare and submit alternate plans. In general, the particular advertising and sales promotion strategy appears to be decided when the brand is launched, and only slight changes are made on a year-to-year basis

TABLE 3.1

Roles in Planning and Budgeting Process: Target and Strategic Planning
(in percent)

Brand Activity	Primarily the Responsibility of:				
	Product Manager	Marketing Management	Functional Specialist	Division/ Corporate Management	Not Done/ No Response
Establish sales targets	63	18	7	11	2
Establish financial goals	30	30	2	33	5
Set other marketing goals	75	14	4	5	2
Situation analysis	82	9	5	2	2
Establish preliminary market- ing budget	62	23	0	9	7
Establish preliminary adver- tising budget	61	14	14	9	2
Establish preliminary sales promotion budget	67	7	19	5	2
Set advertising objectives	68	12	11	4	4
Set sales promotion objectives	81	5	9	0	4

Note: Figures may not total 100 because of rounding.

TABLE 3.2

Roles in Planning and Budgeting Process: Tactical Planning
(in percent)

Brand Activity	Primarily the Responsibility of:					
	Product Manager	Marketing Management	Functional Specialist	Division/ Corporate Management	Outside Agency	Not Done/ No Response
Prepare advertising program	44	5	21	0	21	9
Consumer promotion program	61	2	25	0	6	7
Trade promotion pro- gram	58	4	25	0	6	8
Detailed advertising budget	52	4	26	2	11	4
Detailed consumer pro- motion budget	65	0	25	4	2	5
Detailed trade promo- tion budget	56	2	30	4	12	5
Complete marketing plan	75	12	4	2	2	4
Approve advertising budget	5	35	5	51	0	4
Consumer promotion budget	7	35	7	46	0	5
Trade promotion budget	5	35	7	44	0	9
Final approval of mar- keting plan	4	39	0	53	0	5

Note: Figures may not total 100 because of rounding.

27

(the importance of historical precedent for the allocation decision will be discussed in the next chapter). The only time when there appeared to be some discussion of alternate strategies was when there was a major change in financial goals or overall strategy. This occurred, for example, when it was decided to cut out advertising and "milk" the brand. These occasions are relatively rare.

Ames (1968) has noted a similar failure to consider alternative strategies among marketing planners for industrial products: "Many plans were based on nothing more than straight line extrapolation of the past and on repetition of prior programs" (p. 103).

In virtually every company in the interview study, the discussion at all stages centered on the preparation of the one plan. It was true that advertising agencies and the sales force often presented arguments for increases in advertising or trade promotion, but these were for marginal changes and appeared to have little effect on the final decision. There may also be a considerable amount of informal discussion about different ideas between the planners and their superiors. At best this may be, as one product manager described, "I present my plan and discuss other options I have thought of."

None of these activities could be described as the identification and evaluation of alternative promotional strategies, and, in fact, these options often referred only to alternative programs in a particular area. A frequent procedure was for the planner to define the strategy (that is, the budget and possibly the objectives) for advertising or sales promotion and to ask for submissions on the best execution. Thus, the advertising agency might submit alternate copy themes or, more often, media schedules. In the case of two companies with corporate advertising staffs, these were also asked to submit schedules for the brand. In regard to sales promotion, the interview study found that the product manager discussed alternate tactics with sales promotion and research staff and, in some cases, with the advertising agency. These discussions usually involved such issues as the most appropriate technique for a particular campaign.

In light of these findings, this stage might be better described as "prepare preliminary strategic plans," since it essentially involves the planner's drawing on many sources outside and inside the company to outline a tentative plan for the brand. The sources used might include functional specialists such as advertising, sales promotion, field sales, marketing research, planning, and finance, as well as advertising agency personnel. Their relative roles in the promotional decision will be evaluated in Chapter 5.

Estimate Expected Results

In the APACS formulation, the fifth phase involves the estimation of results for each alternative promotional plan and mix and the

selection of the most appropriate. However, as mentioned in the preceding section, in virtually every company in the interview study there
was only one plan to evaluate. This phase could therefore be better
described as "preparation of the final tactical plan" because, whatever the procedure used to develop the subfunction plans, at this point
the promotional program was integrated.

Among the companies that were interviewed there seemed to be
little effort made to assess the overall results of the plan or even the
results of any part of it. Only one company required the planner to
prepare estimates of the response to advertising, and this was to be
based on an evaluation of the past brand performance. Two companies
prepared detailed expectations of the responses to sales promotion
programs—again based on historical experience.

Two factors probably account for the general failure to estimate
plan results. The first is the "dearth of reliable and precise measures of market response" noted by Robinson and Luck (1964). This
appeared to be a common problem, which reflects, partly, the failure
of many companies to provide for this type of measure and, partly,
the unwillingness of planners to use the information that was available. This problem will be discussed further in Chapter 5.

The other reason for the failure to estimate results could arise
from the inability of the planner to modify sales goals or financial requirements. As one executive commented: "The product manager
has a share goal, a shipment goal and financial guides. It is his goal
to achieve these through the development of an effective marketing
program." A product manager's view was that "only as a last resort"
would he request additional funds. Another noted that it was "easy to
lose budget but very hard to increase it." This, of course, assumes
that the funds provided for promotion would be sufficient to meet the
sales and profit objectives. This budget could be said to be based on
the greater experience of the senior executives who made the initial
decision, but this belief is hard to sustain in the observed cases
where the available funds were reduced but the sales targets remained
the same.

Where targets and budgets are fixed, the major task of the planner is to allocate the available resources (where this has not been
specified in earlier planning stages) and to integrate the various plans.
Therefore, when the subfunction plans are integrated, the emphasis is
likely to be not on the results but on whether the budget requests fit
within the funds available. The process was described by one product
manager: "You add it all up and if you are under the plan you look for
more programs; if you are over, you look for ways to cut."

During the interviews it was found that variations from planned
expenditures could be related to the planner's experience with the
product and the extent to which the preliminary budget was developed.

The greater the experience and the more fully developed the preliminary budget, the less the variance. Regardless of the process, at
this point the allocation decision has been made. The various approaches to this decision are discussed in more detail in the next
chapter.

Table 3.2 shows that among the companies in the mail survey
the functional specialists and the advertising agency are very much
involved in the preparation of detailed plans and budgets for the various promotional elements. However, the product manager is still
most important in all cases and has the major role in the preparation
of the complete marketing plan.

Review and Decision by Management

According to the APACS model, "at this stage management has
the problem of weighing alternatives and including overriding considerations and intangibles prior to adopting final plans and budgets"
(Robinson and Luck 1964, p. 37).

The usual practice among companies in both the Robinson and
Luck study and this investigation was to present only one plan rather
than alternatives. Both studies also found that all planners had secured acceptance at the next highest management level before sub-
mitting a written plan. In the companies that were interviewed, it
appeared that the plans were approved at higher levels with relatively
little change, since they had been prepared within the guidelines laid
down at the beginning of the process. Executives at all levels were
likely to comment on the proposed programs, including advertising
copy, media schedules, and sales promotion activities. However,
these comments were often merely expressions of opinion and did not
necessarily lead to change.

The rare occasions when basic allocations were changed generally seemed to reflect changes in the market environment between
the time the guidelines were established and the time the plans were
submitted. These changes could impact at both division and corporate
levels. The division effort tended to be toward securing additional
funds to support a promising brand or at least the freedom to shift
funds from one brand to the other. The corporate thrust was to require additional contribution from a division in response to a less op-
timistic economic outlook for another division or the corporation as
a whole. The division usually had some freedom in revising its own
budgets to meet this request, although the guidelines were sometimes
specific, as in one corporation where the request was: "We need another half-million dollars from your division. We don't care where
you get it but we suggest you take it from Brand ___."

A review of Table 3.2 indicates that final approval of the marketing plan in the surveyed companies was virtually always at a level higher than the product manager. The marketing manager was important, but in more than half the cases the plan went to division or corporate management for final acceptance.

Feedback of Results and Postaudit

The APACS framework specifies that a plan should include provision for monitoring performance and that regular reviews of results against expectations should be made. The plans investigated in the interview study were similar to those studied by Robinson and Luck in incorporating these provisions and in being regularly reviewed. All plans studied included period sales targets and, sometimes at less frequent intervals, financial objectives. The reviews also drew on information from retail audits and warehouse withdrawals. As has been noted, one company also conducted semiannual surveys of consumer attitudes and purchase behavior, while another made extensive use of consumer panel data to assist in its review procedure. In addition, all companies monitored competitors' advertising expenditures in measured media, and a number subscribed to syndicated services, which provided some information on competitors' sales promotion activities.

Despite the variety of information, the emphasis in most of the review session appeared to be on overall brand sales and profit performance, with little attention paid to the effectiveness of specific promotional programs in contributing to these results. There was some effort to review sales promotion programs, but this often seemed to be nothing more than noting the number of cases that had been shipped during the promotion period. The only two companies that were found to have financial staff at the product manager level did go beyond this in preparing a statement of the financial impact of each sales promotion program; but this was unusual.

Brand shipments were frequently reviewed by the product manager, and regular comparisons were made with the plan. Again, in the two companies that had financial staff attached to the product group, monthly financial reviews were also undertaken. This was particularly important in one company where brands were required to meet their profit objectives each quarter with virtually no room for trading off between quarters. This was unusual and reflected the influence of the division president who had a reputation for "delivering the profit." Most companies evaluated financial performance somewhat less stringently and less frequently during the year, although pressure to meet financial goals increased as the year progressed.

Adapt Program if Required

According to the APACS model, "in the adaptation phase, the decision maker must be prepared to modify goals and subgoals or to alter expenditures if actual experience and competitive interplay so indicate" (Robinson and Luck 1964, p. 37).

These authors reported that most of the consumer goods firms made tactical changes in their plans during the year, a finding that was confirmed among the companies in the interview study. There was also a considerable amount of plan modification reported by the respondents in the survey. Table 3.3 shows that most companies made at least one change equivalent to at least 10 percent of budgeted expenditures for both advertising and sales promotion during the previous financial year. In fact, one-third of the respondents reported three or more changes of this magnitude during that period. The effect of these changes on promotional strategy will be discussed in Chapter 6.

These modifications were strongly influenced by senior management. Table 3.4 showed that senior corporate and division executives initiated practically all of the changes in many of the surveyed companies. However, there is another group of companies— probably those with decentralized profit responsibility—where these executives had practically no influence.

TABLE 3.3

Changes in Budgeted Expenditures
(in percent)

Question: "In the past year, roughly how many changes of 10 percent or more would have been made in budgeted advertising or sales promotion expenditures for established brands?"

Number of Changes	Advertising	Sales Promotion
None	16	28
One of two	46	30
Three or more	35	33
No response	3	9
Total	100	100

TABLE 3.4

Role of Senior Executives in Budget Changes
(percent of those responding)

Question: "Approximately what proportion of these changes would be initiated by senior division or corporate executives?"

Proportion	Corporate[a]	Division[b]
Practically none	33	20
Less than half	14	17
About half	8	11
More than half	8	11
Practically all	36	40

[a]36 responses received.
[b]35 responses received.

VARIATIONS FROM THE APACS MODEL

The preceding discussion has shown that the promotional planning process for established brands is similar in many respects to the process described in the APACS model. Nevertheless, there are several major differences. These are highlighted in Table 3.5, which presents a summary comparison between the APACS model and the promotional planning process found in the companies in the present study. The major differences between the two appear to arise in two main areas: the increased involvement by senior management and the employment of suboptimal planning procedures.

The increased involvement by senior management is seen, first, in the fact that more decisions are being made by them either directly or through the establishment of more formal constraints than appear to be recognized in the model. These constraints include both guidelines for appropriate expense ratios and the classification of products into categories for different strategic treatments. The second form of involvement lies in the increased number of interim approvals that the planning process requires. In the interviews it was found that most planners had to have their initial targets and total budgets approved, as well as the allocations in their preliminary marketing budgets, before proceeding further.

TABLE 3.5

Comparison of APACS Model and Observed Decision Process

APACS	Observed
<u>Define problem and set objectives</u> Define problem associated with promotional actions to be planned and set objectives conforming with overall corporate goals.	<u>Target planning</u> Performance is reviewed, sales and financial goals are set, some budgeting is suggested, and approval is obtained.
<u>Appraise overall situation</u> Undertake comprehensive analysis of market and review of past experience.	<u>Strategic planning</u> A comprehensive analysis of the market is performed, past experience is reviewed, and specific conclusions to guide promotional strategy are developed.
<u>Determine tasks and identify means</u> Determine subgoals to be accomplished and identify appropriate means to achieve these aims.	Subgoals are determined, but many are informal and post hoc. Few alternatives are considered. Preliminary budgets are prepared and approved.
<u>Identify alternate plans and mixes</u> Delineate feasible alternate marketing strategies and promotional mixes and identify additional information required.	Not observed in companies studied.
<u>Estimate expected results</u> Use judgment, experience, and research to forecast results in terms of accepted performance criteria.	<u>Tactical planning</u> Detailed promotional programs are prepared and integrated into the final marketing plan, which is assumed to achieve sales and profit targets already set. Approval is secured at the next level of management.
<u>Assist management in review and decision</u> Line and staff assist management in adopting plans and delegating authority to conduct program.	Approval is given by higher levels of management, provided that constraints are satisfied.
<u>Feed back results and postaudit</u> Collect and communicate data to monitor performance.	<u>Implementation and review</u> This is the same as APACS's. The focus is on performance in relation to financial goals.
<u>Adapt program if required</u> Revise or reaffirm goals, subgoals, and expenditures as necessary.	<u>Adaptation of program</u> Expenditures are changed to ensure that the brand meets financial goals.

The effects of less-than-optimal planning procedures can be seen in the failure to consider alternative promotional mixes and the excessive reliance on what had been done in the past as well as in the various constraints that prevent the decision maker from developing an optimal strategy. These constraints are identified and their impact assessed in Chapter 5.

PLANNING PROCESS FOR
ESTABLISHED BRANDS: A MODEL

In practice the promotional planning process for established brands of consumer nondurable goods in many companies in the study appeared to operate as suggested in Figure 3.2. The process is divided into five stages—three planning phases plus a review phase and adaptation if required. Each of the planning phases is usually centered on the product manager, who works closely with the next highest level of management and draws on various specialists. Approvals are sought after each of the phases. This, of course, is the process in large, multidivision companies using the product manager system. Smaller companies are likely to have a less complex process. Companies that do not use the product manager system were found to rely more on functional specialists and to achieve brand program integration at division management level.

The target planning phase involves a review of the brand's performance and the development of sales forecasts for the coming year. The sales forecasts are used to develop financial targets for the brand, and, together with cost projections, these determine the total promotional budget. Historical patterns of sales, profits, and budgets will be important guides. The budget allocation may be specified, but in any event the constraints that will guide its allocation will be made known. These targets and the budget will be developed by the product manager with substantial input from marketing research, corporate planning (if such a department is established), and finance. The targets and the budget will then be approved at all levels up to corporate management.

The strategic planning phase involves a comprehensive analysis of the product, its markets, and its competition. The result of this analysis will be a series of conclusions regarding the problems and opportunities facing the brand. These are used to guide the preparation of preliminary budgets and the development of goals for the various promotional elements. The budgets will usually include a preliminary allocation of funds for advertising and sales promotion. The situational analysis will be undertaken by the product manager together with the research staff. Financial staff are likely to be involved in

FIGURE 3.2

Promotional Planning Process for Established Brands

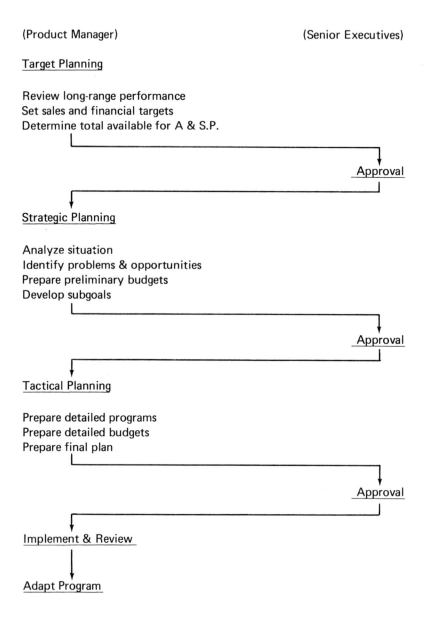

(Product Manager)   (Senior Executives)

Target Planning

Review long-range performance
Set sales and financial targets
Determine total available for A & S.P.

Approval

Strategic Planning

Analyze situation
Identify problems & opportunities
Prepare preliminary budgets
Develop subgoals

Approval

Tactical Planning

Prepare detailed programs
Prepare detailed budgets
Prepare final plan

Approval

Implement & Review

Adapt Program

the preparation of the preliminary budgets. The product manager usually secures approval for his preliminary budget from the executive to whom he reports, and in some cases formal approval may be required at the division level.

Tactical planning is concerned with preparing detailed programs and budgets for each of the promotional elements. These are then integrated into the final plan for the brand. The product manager undertakes this activity together with advertising and sales promotion specialists, representatives of sales management, and the advertising agency. Any of these may be involved in the actual preparation of the detailed plan and/or budget for their area of concern. Informal approval from the product manager's supervisor will be sought for specific programs as they are developed. Final approval will be sought at all levels of the company up to corporate management.

After approval the plan will be implemented and regular reviews undertaken. The product manager will monitor performance on a regular basis with higher-level reviews at monthly or quarterly intervals. The plan will be modified as required by the product manager or at the initiative of higher-level management, depending on the nature of the organization and the extent of the modification. The revised plan will then be implemented.

4

DECISION MODELS FOR ALLOCATING FUNDS
TO ADVERTISING AND SALES PROMOTION

The decision on the allocation of funds between advertising and sales promotion is critical, since it is in this budgeting procedure that brand promotional strategy is crystallized. Despite its importance, this process has received little attention in the academic literature. This chapter examines the applicability of the methods that have been proposed by several authors and discusses other decision procedures identified during the investigation.

The allocation procedure is complex and varied. The decision may be made at various levels in the organization and at several stages in the promotional planning process, as discussed in the preceding chapter. Even when the decision is made and confirmed, the allocation may well be changed as the program is implemented. Under these circumstances it might be expected that a variety of decision models would be employed. The procedures discussed in this chapter include the reliance on a predetermined ratio (most commonly based on historical precedent or strategic classification), the building up of budgets on the basis of relative freedom to fund different elements, competitive parity, and cost minimization.

PREDETERMINED RATIO

Among the companies in which personal interviews were conducted, the most common method for allocating funds to advertising and sales promotion was on the basis of a predetermined ratio. Basically, this involves allocating funds in proportions (for example, 67 percent to advertising, 33 percent to sales promotion) that are largely determined before the planning process for the brand has begun. This approach to the allocation decision was also found in three of the companies studied by Robinson and Luck (1964). It is also noted by Christopher (1972a), who reported that a number of executives in several large corporations in the United Kingdom used "rough rules of thumb" in dividing their total budget between advertising and sales promotion.

However, the most frequent use of a predetermined ratio among the companies in this study was not in the form suggested by these authors. Instead, it occurred in two special applications of the model, namely, the uses of historical precedent and strategic classification. The former may be considered a case of continued reliance on a historically determined ratio, while the adoption of a system of strategic classification typically places severe bounds on the strategic options that a planner can consider. These applications have important implications for the management of promotional strategy and will be discussed separately.

Apart from these applications, the formal use of specified ratios of advertising to sales promotion was not often found among the interviewed companies. In the one case where a ratio was specified (in this case, 60 percent advertising, 40 percent sales promotion), it was recognized that this was a desirable minimum goal rather than an absolute requirement. In establishing this minimum ratio, the company recognized differing strategic impacts of advertising and sales promotion. Executives considered that with a ratio lower than 60 percent advertising no new buyers would be attracted to the brand and that present customers would be vulnerable to competitive activity. An examination of the expenditure patterns for a number of the company's brands produced several examples of variances above and below the specified ratio. Executives commented that these were the result of particular factors in the markets for those brands. The influence of external factors on promotional allocations will be considered in Chapter 7.

The relatively infrequent use of the predetermined ratio in the form suggested in the literature is supported by the finding that companies in the mail survey were much less likely to specify an advertising/sales promotion ratio than to use other guidelines. Table 4.1 shows that only 22 percent of the respondents had the ratio of advertising to sales promotion formally established as a guideline or recommendation. This could indicate a lack of concern for the specific proportion of the budget that is allocated to advertising and sales promotion. On the other hand, it is recognized that the setting of expense ratios for advertising/sales (A/S) and for sales promotion/sales (SP/S) would implicitly establish the ratio of advertising to sales promotion.

A majority of the companies (65 percent) in the survey did report the use of A/S guidelines, but only 43 percent of the respondents

TABLE 4.1

Allocation Guidelines and Recommendations

Question: "In which of the following areas are guidelines or recommendations made by senior executives regarding the allocation of
funds to advertising or sales promotion for established brands?"

Area	Percentage of Respondents (N = 54)
Total dollar amount for advertising and sales promotion	80
Advertising/sales	65
Sales promotion/sales	43
Advertising/sales promotion	22
Classification of brands into strategic clusters for different strategic treatment	48

had recommendations for SP/S. This reinforces a finding of the interview study, namely, that senior executives appeared to be most
concerned with the total budget for advertising and sales promotion
and with the level of advertising in relation to sales. By controlling
these two expenses, senior management can indirectly control the
relationship between advertising and sales promotion. Nevertheless,
it is not a direct control and is perhaps one reason why several executives interviewed were unaware of the actual importance of sales
promotion in the strategy for their brands.

The recommendation of A/S and SP/S ratios did not mean that
they were implemented exactly as required. The interviews suggested
that they were usually seen simply as guides that could be modified
by executive judgment. An example is Pfizer's Hai Karate line of
men's fragrance products where the recommended A/S ratio was
23.2 percent of sales and the SP/S ratio was 21.8 percent of sales
(Ryan and Scott 1977). A review of the actual expenditures (Table
4.2) shows that these guidelines were matched only once in the first
five years.

Guidelines may also operate informally. In two of the companies
interviewed, the planners appeared to have a tacit understanding of
the acceptable proportional allocation. This type of guideline (and the

TABLE 4.2

Hai Karate: Guidelines versus Actual Expenditures
(in percent)

	Advertising/Sales	Sales Promotion/Sales
Guideline	23.2	21.8
Actual		
1968	33.2	25.2
1969	33.0	15.9
1970	23.5	16.5
1971	20.9	20.4
1972	17.6	18.8

Source: Ryan and Scott 1977, p. 93.

use of historical precedent, which is discussed in the next section)
is closest to the predetermined ratio described by Robinson and Luck
(1964). They reported that the ratio was predetermined by the planners themselves and did not mention guidelines proposed by senior
executives. The discovery of such guidelines in this study is strong
evidence of increased involvement by senior management in the promotional planning process.

ROLE OF HISTORICAL PRECEDENT

The single most important guide to the promotional allocation
decision for the planners who were interviewed appeared to be the
expenditure pattern for the brand in the preceding year. In most
cases planners began with a breakdown of expenditures in the previous (current) year and directed their attention to making marginal
changes. As one executive commented, "Most plans are put together
on the basis of historical data." A corporate executive viewed the
process this way: "They [product managers] project dollar and unit
sales for the year then decide whether they are going to spend more
or less than the year before." The effects of this approach can be
seen in Table 4.3. This shows the proportion of the total advertising
and sales promotion budget actually spent on advertising for each
brand over several years. These are not intended to be a representa-

TABLE 4.3

Advertising/Sales Promotion Allocations: Historical Patterns
(in percent)

Year	Detergent (company A)	Toilet Soap (company B)	Paper Product	LIFE Cereal	Lavoris Mouthwash	Unidentified
1	67[a]	63[a]	95[a]	81[b]	76[c]	91[d]
2	65	66	50	82	75	87
3	65	63	42	77	74	76
4	63	62	44	71	61	77
5	66	54	17	60	53	77
6	68	54	23	75	50	76
7	52	n.a.	10	n.a.	53	69
8	62	n.a.	16	n.a.	44	70
9	61	n.a.	19	n.a.	43	70
10	56	n.a.	22	n.a.	n.a.	57

n.a. = not available

[a]Company records.
[b]Case Clearing House 1974 (Quaker Oats: LIFE Cereal).
[c]Davis and Shapiro 1974 (Vick Chemical Company).
[d]Nielsen Researcher 1976.

Note: The figures represent the percentage of total advertising and sales promotion allocated to advertising for each brand.

tive sample of brands; indeed, it would be difficult to draw such a sample since many companies do not have extensive records in this form. The brands were selected from a limited number with at least six years history to provide a cross section of different companies and different product categories.

The history of these brands clearly shows the effects of historical precedent on the allocations to advertising and sales promotion. Among the six brands there are a total of 45 possible interperiod comparisons. In more than half of these (25), the year-to-year change in the advertising allocation is less than ±5 percent. In 13 cases the change is zero or ±1 percent. The remaining year-to-year changes are equally divided between moderate shifts (±5 to 9 percent) and major changes in promotional strategy (±10 percent or more). In fact, some of these major changes arise from a temporary change in strategy that is immediately returned to the historical pattern in the following year (for example, Detergent, year 7; LIFE Cereal, year 5). The other changes represent permanent shifts in strategy, which are once again followed by periods of stability.

The maintenance of promotional allocations over a period of years is reinforced by the presence of formal or informal guidelines as to acceptable ratios. It is also likely that there will be greater variation in allocations in the first years of a new brand.

Disturbances in the pattern arise both from factors within the company and from changes in the external environment. The nature and effects of these will be considered in more detail in later chapters. An example of the powerful role of precedent was found in one company where the proposed allocation was checked against the historic allocation and explanations sought for any variation.

All individuals involved in the promotional planning process are likely to be similarly limited by what was done in the past. As one senior sales promotion executive described it, their decision process hinges on three questions: "How much did we have to spend last year? What have we got to spend this year? How will we cut it up?" Even where executives submit requests for alternate allocations, they are likely to be in terms of increments over previous years rather than major changes.

It is not surprising that planners seek only marginal changes in promotional strategy from year to year. March and Simon (1958) have commented on the difficulties faced by decision makers in foreseeing the outcome of various actions owing to the uncertainties of the environment and the complex interrelationships among the elements of strategy. This is likely to be especially true in decisions about alternative promotional allocations where there are many options among potentially interactive variables and uncertain consequences in terms of consumer and competitor responses. This may result in "tunnel vision" among many planners, especially in one case as reported by Ames (1968) in his study of industrial marketing planning:

> In one company when each planner was asked by top management to outline alternative strategies . . . the request drew a complete blank. The planners were so locked into their accustomed way of thinking about their markets that they could not conceive of a different approach that made any commercial sense at all. [P. 103]

Even though they were studying the planning process for new products, Robinson and Luck (1964) also found evidence of limited efforts to seek alternatives in the planners' "tendency to conduct search in the neighborhood of recently pursued courses of action" (p. 58).

STRATEGIC CLASSIFICATION

In recent years the Boston Consulting Group (1970) has developed and publicized the concept of the product portfolio approach to strategic planning. This basically involves the classification of a company's brands into different groups based on their market share and growth potential. Each group of products is then associated with a different marketing strategy.

This approach appears to have been adopted in some degree by a sizable number of companies. Two of the companies in the interview study had incorporated the concept in their strategic planning, and the survey found almost half of the respondents reporting the classification of brands into strategic clusters for different strategic treatments (see Table 4.1). The concept has important implications for promotional planning because it was found to affect not only the total funds available for advertising and sales promotion but also their allocation. These effects will be discussed in the next chapter.

However, the adoption of the product portfolio also affects the method by which allocations are made. Once a product is placed within a category, then its promotional budget must conform to the guidelines established for that category. For products with relatively high market shares and good growth potential, executives have considerable freedom in deciding the level and mix of promotion effort. Products that have little potential growth, however, are in a category where the level and mix of promotional effort are allowed little variation from year to year. In all categories historical spending patterns were used as a guide; so this tended to reinforce the importance of "budgeting by precedent."

In the two companies the promotional allocation for the brands was included in the long-term plans. Thus the ratio was established and the planner could do little but make marginal changes. It was found that there was more freedom to change in practice than in theory, but both companies curtailed this, in the planning stages at least, by requiring top management approval of the preliminary budget. It was possible to change the category to which a brand had been assigned, but this required detailed analysis and extensive justification.

BUILDUP APPROACH

Robinson and Luck (1964) describe the "building up" of a promotional budget by the planner who begins with the most fixed element (usually trade promotion) and ends with the most flexible (usually media advertising). In most cases this was done within the total budget constraint, but two planners developed an ideal budget and then worked back to satisfy the constraint. A similar procedure is suggested by Winkler (1972), although no empirical evidence is presented.

The buildup method was found to be the most common method of budget allocation among the companies studied by Robinson and Luck. However, among the planners in the companies interviewed for the present study, this method appeared to be rarely used as the primary procedure for establishing promotional allocations. In only one company did a planner report preparing an initial budget incorporating an ideal strategy. This he described as his "Oh, wow" budget, the preparation of which was immediately followed by action to decide "which of these programs can I cut out?" Even this planner commented that after working on the brand for the three years since it had been marketed, his ideal budget was usually close to the final budget. In no other instance was the buildup approach found to be the main method utilized.

The buildup method was important in combination with other methods, especially in making marginal revisions to meet budget constraints. As was discussed earlier, most allocations in the companies that were studied were made on the basis of revisions of the previous year's expenditures. There were cases where, because of changes in costs or other program requirements, trade-offs had to be made to meet the total budget constraint. These did not usually involve significant portions of the budget, and the planner made the decision on the basis of the program's perceived importance in helping the brand meet performance goals. This was also the case with budget revisions after plan approval, which will be discussed in Chapter 6. The other factor that influenced the trade-off decision was the relative power of the planner as compared with the managers in the functional areas. This issue will be considered in the next chapter.

The main reason for the apparently less important role of the buildup method among the companies studied may be the fact that the focus was on promotional planning for established brands as distinct from new brands. In the case of new brands, the planner may have relatively little information on which to base the allocation decision. One way of reducing this uncertainty is to provide for the essential elements first and to allocate the remaining funds to programs that are seen as less vital. This procedure is encouraged by factors such as the demands of retailers for allowances and other support as a requirement for stocking a new brand. On the other hand, all participants in the promotional planning process for established brands at least have the record of past expenditures, and budget planning is likely to begin from this base.

A second reason for the less important role of the buildup method could be the apparently greater degree of involvement in the allocation decision by senior management. In the companies studied, the planners appeared to be more subject to restrictions imposed by senior management than in the cases observed by Robinson and Luck. The role of senior management will be discussed in the following chapter.

COMPETITIVE PARITY METHOD

As proposed by Winkler (1972) and endorsed by Engel, Wales, and Warshaw (1975), the competitive parity method requires planners to calculate the allocations used by competitors and to adjust their own allocations accordingly. These authors do not present empirical evidence to indicate how widely this procedure is used.

In the interviewed companies, competitors' allocations were certainly taken into account in the budget decision, but they could not be said to be a primary determinant in any instance. The main impact of competitors' activities was on levels of particular elements of promotion rather than on the overall allocation. In one company a planner endeavored to maintain a high level of advertising to counter a competitor who was spending heavily in this area. In another case a planner felt that she had to increase her trade promotion spending to match a competitor who was having some success at that level. In the market described by Weber (1973), the adoption of a sales promotion-oriented strategy by one brand led the two larger brands in the market to change their allocation, although none matched that of the originating brand.

In fact, in none of these companies did the planner try to match the overall allocation used by competitors. One reason for this was the practical difficulty of determining the actual allocation used by a competitor. There were published estimates of advertising spending, but little was available on sales promotion. A syndicated service to estimate consumer promotion expenditures began operation in selected markets in 1975. However, trade promotions were still largely an unknown quantity, although manufacturers were asked to match trade allowances offered by competitors. Under these conditions it is unlikely that competitive allocation can have more than a general effect on spending levels.

MINIMUM-COST METHOD

Boyd and Massey (1972) conclude that in many cases marketing decision makers look for the least-cost strategy that will achieve a defined objective. This avoids "the problem of finding the optimal budget level in relation to sales" in favor of "the problem of finding the lowest-cost way of attaining a specific target." Winkler (1972) suggests that in some companies this method is used to determine the promotional allocation as planners seek to exploit the synergistic relationship between advertising and sales promotion.

There was little evidence of this approach in the companies studied. It may have been the intention of some senior executives to encourage this type of planning when they specified a sales target and a total promotional budget. However, there were no signs that this total had been determined to be the minimum cost, no executives gave this as the reason for setting limits on expenditures, and the planners did not operate in the expected fashion (that is, search for optimal allocations). As has been noted, there was little effort to seek alternative allocations, and planners invariably spent all the funds that were available. It could be said that the planners behaved very much in the fashion described by March and Simon (1958) as "satisficing" when they accepted the first allocation that satisfied their requirements, regardless of its optimality. Robinson and Luck (1964) came to a similar conclusion.

OPTIMIZING ALLOCATION DECISIONS

The preceding discussion emphasizes that advertising/sales promotion allocation decisions are largely made on the basis of historical precedent and various rules of thumb with little regard for optimality. In fact, there was a general concern that the budget be distributed in the most effective way, and many decisions incorporated a good deal of experience. Several planners who were interviewed reported making small changes in their allocations from year to year to improve the effectiveness of their promotional strategy in the light of their evolving understanding of the market. The major obstacles to further efforts to develop optimal allocations appeared to arise from the planners' reluctance to consider major changes from past practice and various organizational constraints as well as the planners' perception that the task would be too complex and therefore impossible.

Nevertheless, several planners indicated that they had taken further steps to aid their allocation decision making. Their efforts were in two areas, experimentation and modeling. The experiments that were reported usually involved regional tests of different alloca-

FIGURE 4.1

Allocation Decision Process for Established Brands

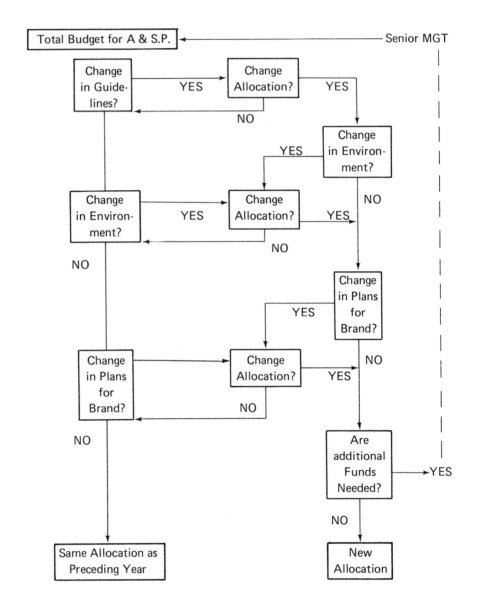

tions, including the elimination of trade promotions, and tests of different weights of advertising and/or consumer promotions. Unfortunately, in the few tests of this type that were described, the results were often obscured by methodological problems and only informally incorporated into decision making.

Several other experiments were reported using a laboratory situation. Two companies had conducted tests at the AdTel facility, which operates matched panels of cable television homes in two cities. These experiments were directed toward testing the interactive relationship (if any) between advertising and sales promotion and the effects of differing weights of advertising with various consumer promotions (an example of this type of study is discussed by Sunoo and Lin [1978]). The results of these experiments were directly incorporated into promotional strategy for the brands involved.

In the mail survey less than one-fourth of the respondents reported the use of models to aid their allocation of the total promotional budget (see Table 5. 7). In most cases these probably refer to the Hendry Corporation's market simulation model. Three of the companies interviewed used this model and were able to test alternate strategies.

A different and potentially interesting use of models to aid the budget decision is described by Singer and DeBruicker (1975a) in the General Foods Corporation Tang case study. Here, multiple regression techniques were used to develop models of the effects of advertising and sales promotion on brand sales. These were used to determine optimal levels and allocations for the total advertising and sales promotion budget. One company in the interview study was moving to develop a model of this type to aid sales promotion decisions.

Despite these efforts, the results appeared to have little impact on planners' decisions in the companies that were studied. In some cases the planners who were interviewed were not aware that the information existed or did not feel it was relevant. In one company the simulation model was reserved for use on strategy for new products.

CONCLUSION

While different companies use various models to allocate funds between advertising and sales promotion, the most common procedure is that described in the flow chart in Figure 4. 1. This reflects the observed behavior that, unless there are major changes in the market environment, the allocation will be similar to that made in the preceding year. It need not be exactly the same, but in most cases the allocation for the coming year will involve only marginal changes. Major shifts in the proportion of funds devoted to advertising and sales promotion are likely to occur only infrequently for most established brands.

5

IMPACT OF ORGANIZATIONAL FACTORS
ON PROMOTIONAL PLANNING

The particular structure and operating characteristics of an organization will have a significant impact on promotional strategy as it will on the other strategic choices that are made. In their study Robinson and Luck (1964) paid a good deal of attention to these internal factors, which they divided into three groups. These were the position in the organization of the person who made the decisions on promotional strategy, the degree to which the decision maker was free to develop such a strategy, and the extent to which information and planning were coordinated. Each of these areas was investigated in this study, and this chapter reports the findings and discusses some of the ways in which current practices inhibit the development of effective strategy. The relationships between the product manager and the various specialists (sales, advertising, sales promotion) are also examined.

POSITION OF THE DECISION MAKER

To understand the promotional planning process, it is important to describe the position of the decision maker(s) within the organization and to identify other executives who may be involved. This is not a simple matter. The company interviews demonstrated that not only did organizations make the critical allocation decision at different levels but that executives within the organization themselves had different perceptions of the relevant decision maker.

In their study Robinson and Luck (1964) addressed this problem by focusing on the individuals who made several key decisions. These included decisions on the sales and profit goals for the brand, the total budget for the brand, and the allocation of funds to advertising and sales promotion. Each of these questions was incorporated in the survey instrument, and the first part of this chapter will draw on these responses together with information from the interview study to identify the decision maker and the other executives involved.

Robinson and Luck were particularly concerned with identifying the key individual who "assembles and integrates the alternative promotional tools into a unified strategy" (p. 32). The latter part of this chapter will deal with issues of coordination and integration and will conclude with a review of the role of the product manager in allocation decisions.

Establishing Brand Goals

Table 5.1 shows that among the surveyed companies there are substantial differences between the decision-making roles for the establishment of brand sales goals and brand financial goals. In both cases decisions are made at all levels from corporate executives to the product manager, but it is obvious that executives above the product manager level are considerably more likely to set financial requirements. Financial goals were established by marketing managers or higher-level executives in two-thirds of the companies that responded to this question. Sales goals were decided at these levels in slightly less than one-third of the cases.

In some companies these may be set at the highest level. For example, at Alberto-Culver the president reportedly views goal setting for individual brands as a major responsibility: "My primary responsibility to my managers is to set guidelines for the sales and profit results of the products for which they are responsible" (Clarke and Marshall 1973).

Even where the product manager appears to have a greater role, both the interviews and the survey showed that, although the product manager may often set the sales target and profit goal for the brand, in virtually every case these were subject to approval at higher levels. It was found that usually this approval had to be secured during the preliminary or target planning phase described earlier and before annual planning could begin. The usual practice appeared to be for the proposed figures to be accepted as long as they were within a reasonable range. In regard to sales targets, one executive commented, "These are established by the product manager as long as market research doesn't say they are absurd." However, these could be changed (as discussed earlier) in order to meet corporate financial requirements or to reflect changing strategic priorities.

Financial goals and sales targets were separated on the questionnaire because the interviews found that product managers were

TABLE 5.1

Roles in the Allocation Decision
(in percent)

Brand Activity	Primarily the Responsibility of:				
	Product Manager	Marketing Management	Functional Specialist	Division/ Corporate Management	Not Done/ No Response
Establish sales targets	63	18	7	11	2
Establish financial goals	30	30	2	33	5
Establish preliminary marketing budget	61	23	0	9	7
Establish preliminary advertising budget	61	14	14	9	2
Establish preliminary sales pro- motion budget	67	7	19	5	2
Approve advertising budget	5	35	5	51	4
Approve consumer promotion budget	7	35	7	46	5
Approve trade promotion budget	5	35	7	44	9
Final approval of marketing plan	4	39	0	53	5

Note: Figures may not total 100 because of rounding.

generally involved in preparing sales forecasts but that the process
for setting financial goals was more complex. In some of the companies in which interviews were conducted, product managers were
not asked to set financial goals. In other cases they proposed these
goals but without any idea of corporate requirements. In both these
situations an overall financial goal would be decided on (usually at the
corporate level), and then individual brand requirements would be
determined. Financial goals seemed to be least likely to be changed
when they had been incorporated in the long-term plan for a brand that
was performing up to expectations. Even in these cases, however,
the original long-term goals had been established by senior management and not by the product manager. In most of the companies
studied, therefore, the product manager did not make decisions on
the profit goals for the brand and was severely limited in establishing sales targets.

In preparing the sales and profit forecasts, the product manager
consulted with other executives from different departments. These
included marketing research, corporate planning (in one company interviewed there was a special forecasting department at the corporate
level), finance, sales management, and purchasing (estimates of future material costs). Their primary input was information relating
to likely future sales and costs.

Determining the Marketing Budget

During the interviews it was found that in most cases the marketing budget for consumer nondurables was largely concerned with
advertising and sales promotion expenditures. For one company these
accounted for 90 percent of the direct marketing costs that were at-
tributed to the brand. It was also found that the total funds available
for these activities were determined (as Kotler [1972] and others have
noted) as a residual after providing for profits and other costs. This
meant that in most cases the decision on the financial goals for the
brand also determined the total advertising and sales promotion budget for that brand. Thus, in the companies that were interviewed,
the role of the product manager in establishing the total budget for
the brand emerged as similar to that described by Clewett and Stasch
(1975)—they had a "strong voice" but did not have final control.

The survey responses suggest that the product manager had a
greater role when it came to allocating these funds. Table 5.1 shows
that the product manager was most likely to be responsible for establishing the preliminary marketing budget, which would usually include some allocation of funds to advertising and sales promotion.
However, during the interviews it was discovered that in most cases

this preliminary budget would be approved informally by the product manager's superior and possibly by one higher level before detailed planning began. The interviews also revealed that financial staff were heavily involved at this stage, although their role was essentially advisory. They acted to ensure that product managers were aware of the implications of their decisions in regard to the available funds and the financial goals for the brand. In some cases they also provided information upward to the division and corporate financial staff as an input to their planning for the division and corporation.

Allocating Funds to Advertising
and Sales Promotion

In the interview study the decision on the allocation of funds to advertising and sales promotion was generally made in conjunction with the development of the preliminary marketing budget. This initial allocation was crystallized in the preparation of preliminary budgets for advertising and sales promotion. Among the companies that were interviewed, these budgets were most likely to be prepared by the product manager, although, again, this was subject to approval by senior executives.

This finding is supported by the respondents in the survey. Table 5.1 shows that in more than 60 percent of these companies the product manager was responsible for preparing the preliminary budgets for advertising and sales promotion. However, the product manager clearly does not have the responsibility for approving these budgets, and even the marketing manager is overshadowed by division and corporate executives who have responsibility in half the cases. In his study Banks (1973) also found that product managers were most likely to have responsibility for preparing advertising and sales promotion budgets and that division management had a major role in their approval.

During the company interviews it was found that functional specialists in sales management, advertising, and sales promotion could be consulted at this stage and that some might even be asked to outline budgets for their area. However, their involvement was more likely after the preliminary budgets had been approved when they operated within the spending limits set by product management. This did not prevent the specialists from trying, usually unsuccessfully, to increase the allocation to their particular area. In companies that did not employ the product manager system, these executives were usually responsible for all the budget preparation for their functional area. The relationship between product managers and functional specialists is further discussed later in this chapter.

There is also some indication from Table 5.1 that product managers in the surveyed companies were marginally more likely to be responsible for sales promotion budgeting than for advertising. Further evidence of this is provided in the lower proportion of respondent companies that had guidelines for sales promotion spending than for advertising. As discussed earlier, both Lucas (1972) and Clewett and Stasch (1975) reported that product managers had a greater role in sales promotion decision making than in advertising. The reasons for this may include the relatively lesser concern that senior executives appear to have for sales promotion as compared with advertising, the smaller amounts involved in individual programs (compared with advertising), and the less important role of outside agencies.

Coordination and Integration

As can be seen from Table 5.1, the product manager is most likely to be responsible for integrating all promotional activities in drawing up the complete marketing plan for the brand. This confirms the earlier discussion of other studies that concluded that planning was a major function of the product manager. However, it is interesting to note that the product manager is rarely involved in approving the final brand plan. Once again, division and corporate management takes this responsibility in more than half the cases, with the bulk of the rest being the task of senior marketing executives.

Coordination at an earlier stage in the promotional planning process is also important. If companies are to capitalize on the synergistic relationship between advertising and sales promotion, then their budgets must be developed in a coordinated manner. The interviews suggested that this could be accomplished by having one individual, usually the product manager, responsible for budgeting both advertising and sales promotion.

An analysis of the results from the survey (Table 5.2) show that decisions on the advertising and sales promotion budget were made by the same individual in most (86 percent) of the respondent companies. In 70 percent of these cases, this individual was the product manager, which reinforces the importance of this executive in the promotional allocation decision. In the 12 cases where this individual was not the product manager, it was usually the next-highest-level marketing executive, a division or corporate officer, or a committee.

However, the extent of the coordination appears to diminish when other activities that could be seen as essential to an effective promotional strategy are added. Table 5.2 shows that in only 39 percent of the surveyed companies was the same person responsible for establishing the preliminary marketing budget as well as the individual

TABLE 5.2

Coordination of Advertising and Sales Promotion Budgeting
(in percent)

Same Person Responsible for:	Percentage of Respondents (N = 56)	Product Manager	Marketing Manager	Other
Preliminary advertising and sales promotion budget	86	70	17	13
Above plus preliminary marketing budget	39	77	23	0
Above plus establishing financial goals	29	75	25	0

budgets. This probably reflects the fact mentioned earlier—namely, that in some companies the establishing of the preliminary budget sets the allocation for advertising and sales promotion and therefore provides coordination at that level.

When responsibility for establishing the budget is incorporated, the proportion of companies where the same person sets goals and allocates the budget drops to 23 percent. In fact, as many as three different people were involved in these four related activities, with the average being just below two.

Changing Role of the Product Manager
in Promotional Decisions

The role of the product manager in the promotional planning process has undoubtedly changed in the 13 years since the Robinson and Luck study. There appears to be a greater number of formal and informal constraints imposed by senior management. These are reflected in the guidelines and recommendations on appropriate allocations as well as in an increased requirement for interim approvals, which was not recognized as a factor in the earlier study. There are also informal constraints—the interviews revealed that product managers usually consult with their superiors once a day and often more frequently during the planning period. The training that the individual product manager has had in a company also has a substantial influence on their decisions. The president of Alberto-Culver has described the effect in his company: "For example, I receive copies of every commercial which a product manager might want to use for his product; because he has been trained to think the way we do, I accept 99 out of every hundred" (Clarke and Marshall 1973).

Given the existence of these and other constraints, the product manager cannot be said to have overall responsibility for brand advertising and sales promotion. However, the product manager retains some important functions. As was clear from the survey results, the product manager has the major role in coordinating promotional activities for the brand. Further, in the interviews it was found that the product manager is the individual who is most likely to initiate strategies for the brand and who has the opportunity to negotiate changes in allocations, even when guidelines are established. These three factors mean that the product manager is the individual most actively involved in the promotional allocation decision and the person who is likely to play the most important role in that decision. In fact, while higher-level executives have more authority, it is likely to be exercised in a reactive fashion rather than as a positive determinant of promotional strategy. One group product manager described the relationship this way: "My role is basically to ensure the correctness of brand objectives, strategy and tactics—to see that the programs are consistent with the corporate and market environment."

Thus, the product manager may propose the strategy (within many of these constraints) and a superior will act to provide a check. One thing has not changed since the Robinson and Luck study: a proposed strategy and budget are likely to be approved at all levels provided that they satisfy the established constraints.

In the companies in which interviews were conducted, it was found that the degree to which these constraints operated appeared to depend on the degree of decentralization within the company. The product manager was likely to have considerably more freedom in a highly decentralized company where the individual (or group) had a greater degree of profit responsibility. One marketing manager in a decentralized company suggested the effect of this when he commented that the division president "has to have a pretty strong objection to make the product group change," although he added that the president could force a trade-off with the group. Product managers in decentralized companies also appeared to have greater experience than their counterparts in more centralized organizations.

The question of experience is important because the interviews further suggested that the product manager's degree of independence in making promotional decisions was related to this factor. This is similar to the conclusion of Robinson and Luck that the more experienced product managers relied less on assistance from functional specialists. As will be discussed in the next section, it was found that the product manager appears to have a greater degree of authority over functional specialists than in the earlier study—a situation that could be partly explained by the greater degree of knowledge about established brands than new brands.

DEGREE OF DECISION FREEDOM

From the discussion in the preceding section, it is obvious that the individual most involved in decisions on promotional strategy for the brand is the product or brand manager. This was the conclusion reached by Robinson and Luck in their study, although they recognized a number of constraints that restricted the freedom of the product manager to develop promotional strategy. A review of the literature since their study was undertaken has suggested that in recent years the role of the product manager has been increasingly constrained. This section examines some of these constraints as they relate to promotional strategy decisions. In particular, it considers restrictions on resources and allocation, restrictions on techniques, and relationships between the product manager and the functional areas.

Resource Restrictions

The most common constraint on the product manager's freedom to develop promotional strategy was found, in both the interviews and the survey, to be the absence of control over the total advertising and sales promotion budget for the brand. This restriction has also been observed by Robinson and Luck (1964), Buell (1973), and Clewett and Stasch (1975).

The questionnaire included a specific section on the guidelines or recommendations that were made by senior executives regarding the allocation of funds to advertising or sales promotion for established brands. The responses to this section were presented in Table 4.1. Of those who responded to this question, 80 percent reported that such guidelines were established for the total budget for advertising and sales promotion. This confirms the earlier discussion regarding the fact that, given that advertising and sales promotion funds are computed as residuals, the determination of financial goals for a brand by senior management also decides the total budget for these promotional activities.

The level at which the total promotional budget was set reflected a number of factors including the previous history of the brand, the relative importance of the brand to the company, and senior management's view of its future. If a brand was particularly important to the company, then resources would be less likely to be limited, regardless of the sales potential. This is an extension of Hurwood's (1968) conclusion that brands that were more important in terms of sales or profits were more likely to have advertising support.

It is interesting to note that during the interviews some executives reported that the level at which the total budget was set influenced the allocation of funds to advertising or sales promotion. The general effect was that, when the total budget was small, most of the funds were allocated to sales promotion, with the converse being true—although to a lesser extent—with a large appropriation. One executive justified this approach on the grounds that the effective "threshold" for sales promotion activities was reached at a lower level of expenditure than that for advertising.

As well as restricting total budgets, many companies were found to place constraints on the way funds were allocated. The survey revealed that almost two-thirds of the respondents had guidelines or recommendations regarding an appropriate ratio of advertising to sales and that more than one-third had similar constraints on the ratio of sales promotion to sales (see Table 4.1). Thus, in most companies the allocation to advertising and sales promotion could be determined since it would only require specification of any two of the three constraints mentioned.

However, the impact on the allocation decision for an individual brand was not as great as might be expected. In a number of the interviewed companies, the advertising/sales (A/S) and sales promotion/sales (SP/S) ratios were set for the corporation and possibly for the division as a whole, but managers within the division had some freedom in varying the ratios for their individual brands. Second, there appeared to be less pressure to conform to A/S and AP/S ratios as compared with the emphasis on meeting financial targets. In many of these companies, these ratios were nothing more than guidelines, and product managers were free to negotiate alternate strategies, provided that the total budget was not affected. An example of this was discussed in Chapter 4 in relation to the actual spending pattern for Hai Karate.

It is interesting to note that survey respondents were more likely to have established guidelines for advertising spending than for sales promotion. This suggests that product managers are likely to have more decision freedom in relation to sales promotion than to advertising. This may also reflect an orientation toward advertising as the major promotional expense item for many brands. In fact, as reported in Chapter 1, most companies marketing consumer nondurable goods are likely to be spending more on sales promotion than on advertising for most of their brands. In the interview study, there were several instances of executives not being aware of the extent to which sales promotion expenditures exceeded advertising for some of the brands in their group. This was usually due to a failure to record all items of sales promotion expenditure (for example, revenue lost from temporary price reductions) or to a failure to combine all items of sales promotion expenditure in a single account.

This apparent lack of concern for the relation of sales promotion to advertising in some companies is reflected in the relatively small proportion of respondents (21 percent) who reported senior management guidelines on the ratio of advertising to sales promotion. This low proportion also suggests that product managers may have a certain amount of freedom to change the allocation of funds within the total budget constraint. Even where these guidelines are established, they are likely to be readily modified as has been shown.

Restriction on Techniques

Robinson and Luck (1964) found that within the total budget constraint product managers had "wide freedom in deciding the promotional means" although they did note three cases of restrictions in prior commitments to certain media. This type of constraint was also found in the interview study, although it varied considerably by company. In one case the corporation took major sponsorships in three national events during the year, and most brands were required to participate in both advertising and sales promotion activities related to these events. For one or two smaller brands, this was likely to absorb their total advertising budget, and it certainly restricted the options of the remainder. At the other extreme, another corporation deliberately avoided this type of sponsorship. In this organization in the rare cases where such activity was undertaken, it was viewed as a corporate expense and budgeted accordingly.

Among the companies that were interviewed, the most common corporate restraint in this area appeared to be a general preference for advertising over sales promotion. The basis for this preference was sometimes rather tenuous and seemed to reflect a management conviction that advertising was "nicer" or "better for the company image." In one company this led to a severe restriction on sales promotion activities, but this restriction was relaxed in the face of increasingly competitive markets during the late 1960s. Of course, there were companies where executives provided more substantial reasons for their preference, including the previously mentioned company that stressed the importance of advertising to emphasize product benefits to attract new customers and keep existing ones.

Other restrictions related to the use of certain types of promotion. During the interviews several executives reported preference for consumer-oriented promotion over trade-oriented promotion, because it was felt that the company had more control and could ensure that the whole of the benefit was passed on to the consumer. In fact, there has been a general movement toward consumer promotion at the expense of trade promotions. Trade-oriented promotions were often seen as a form of subsidy or a "cost of doing business," and the basis for planning was sometimes expressed as "how little do we have to spend to stay in the market." Companies might also restrict certain types of consumer-oriented promotion, such as price promotions, for fear of damaging the brand image.

One other restriction is of interest in the case of a company that relied heavily on a "family" brand strategy. Here the use of advertising for individual products was sometimes limited because senior executives felt that the image had been sufficiently well established by other brand advertising.

RELATIONS WITH FUNCTIONAL SPECIALISTS

Another potential constraint that affects advertising and sales promotion strategy is the relative degree of influence that executives in functional areas—especially the areas of sales management, advertising, and sales promotion—have over the product manager and promotional strategy. Robinson and Luck (1964) found that the product manager generally had a lower degree of influence and authority compared with these executives, particularly sales executives and to a lesser extent those in advertising. Despite this, they concluded that promotional decisions were made largely independently by the product manager. Recent studies have confirmed the lack of influence over the personal-selling function but have suggested that the product manager has taken a more prominent role in advertising planning than described in the earlier study. This section will review the relationship between the product manager and each of the three functional areas in relation to the promotional allocation decision.

Relationship with Sales Management

Robinson and Luck (1964) found that sales executives had a strong influence over all aspects of the promotional decision-making process. Their "dominant voice appeared to be most effective in the establish-

TABLE 5.3

Functional Specialists: Roles in Advertising and Sales Promotion Planning
(in percent)

Question: "For each of the following departments, indicate the role of their personnel in advertising and/or sales promotion planning for established brands."

Department	Not Involved	Consulted	Prepares Proposals	Approves	Number Responding
Advertising planning					
Sales management	35	58	0	8	52
Corporate advertising	23	40	27	10	30
Division advertising	4	16	52	28	25
Corporate sales promotion	43	24	33	0	21
Division sales promotion	41	18	32	9	34
Advertising agency	5	32	57	5	54
Sales promotion agency	62	17	17	4	23
Sales promotion planning					
Sales management	4	65	10	19	48
Corporate advertising	39	22	30	9	23
Division advertising	16	21	32	32	19
Corporate sales promotion	19	31	50	0	16
Division sales promotion	0	21	64	14	28
Advertising Agency	20	60	20	0	40
Sales promotion agency	10	45	45	0	20

Note: Figures may not total 100 because of rounding.

ment of policies limiting the promotional and advertising tools that would be used, and in the higher level influence on determination of total budgets" (p. 111).

Nowhere in this study was this degree of dominance found. It was apparent in the interviews that the product manager had little influence over personal-selling function, which in some cases forces at least a minimum sales promotion effort to win sales-force support for the brand. It also appeared that sales management had little direct influence on brand promotional strategy. There were only two areas where sales executives might have significant influence—the trade promotion budget and program and the total budget for the brand. Even in these instances, their impact was likely to be limited.

Sales management's role in the advertising and sales promotion planning process was assessed in the survey, and the results are presented in Table 5.3. This shows that in 35 percent of the respondent companies, sales management is not involved at all in advertising planning and has only a consultative role at best. Sales management has the greater involvement in sales promotion planning, but again the role is essentially consultative. Even where the degree of involvement is greater, this may not mean a substantial impact on promotional budgets, as was found in one company where the sales department had to provide formal approval of the promotional program, targets, and budget. Even in this situation, a senior sales executive noted that their main concern was with the trade promotion budget and that, while this was "somewhat negotiated," he found that he and the product manager "rarely disagreed." He reported that the sales department could get some changes in the form of promotions that were planned but that changes in funding were very rare.

Sales executives in another company reported a similar arrangement with the product manager establishing the trade promotion budget for the brand and then negotiating with the sales department over marginal changes. Both this company and another in the interview study reported that sales management made recommendations for trade promotion support for each brand in each market but that the final decision was with marketing management. However, in all these cases it was likely that the product manager would consider sales-force needs in setting the budget.

One interesting development that was revealed in the interviews was the change in control of trade promotion programs in recent years. Two companies reported that they had tried to centralize control of trade promotions in the hands of the product manager but had found that this reduced effectiveness because of the variations from market to market. Both of these companies were now giving their sales department more freedom to plan and to implement their own trade promotion in local markets. The budget was established by the product manager, who also had to approve proposed programs, but otherwise the sales force had some degree of independence. One well-known company that was not interviewed had reportedly even appointed a number of "market managers" to coordinate the sales promotion activities in different geographical areas.

The sales department did have some impact on the total promotional budget in terms of securing additional funds during the year. Product managers who were interviewed commented that they were able to ignore the "random requests" for additional support from sales executives but reported several occasions where the total budget had been increased as a result of direct appeals to top management from the sales department. These occasions were usually to help a brand that was facing unexpectedly strong competitive pressure.

Relationship with Advertising

As has already been mentioned, the expansion of the product manager system had a concomitantly negative effect on the role of the advertising specialist. This was confirmed in the survey where less than half the respondents reported having an executive with specialist responsibilities for advertising at either corporate or division level (see Table 5.4).

The advertising specialist's role in the promotional budgeting decision also appeared to be a minor one, and in none of the interviewed companies did they have a dominant voice in advertising budgeting. One marketing executive described his company's advertising department as being "resources to draw on if we need them," and a vice-president of corporate advertising similarly recognized that "it all begins with marketing." In Table 5.3 it can be seen that the primary role of the corporate advertising department in advertising is consultative (40 percent of the respondents), while the division departments are more actively involved in preparing advertising proposals. This is supported by responses to questions on planning activities (Table 3.2), which showed that advertising specialists were more likely to be responsible for preparing the advertising program or the detailed advertising budget rather than for establishing targets or budgets or approving the final promotional plan.

In most companies in which interviews were conducted, the major function of the advertising department appeared to be in the planning, reviewing, and buying of media. This was usually done in association with the advertising agency for the brand. The advertising specialist in some companies was also asked to sit in on major copy presentations by the agency. In these cases their influence "depends on the person there," with a perceived expert having a poten-

TABLE 5.4

Advertising and Sales Promotion Specialists: Number and Location

Question: "Does your organization have an executive or executives with specialist responsibilities for advertising and/or sales promotion activities?"

		Present Position Established		
	Total	Before 1960	1960-70	Since 1970
At corporate level				
Advertising only	13	5	5	3
Sales promotion only	12	6	1	5
Advertising and sales promotion	9	2	3	4
Total	34	13	9	12
At division level				
Advertising only	15	5	6	4
Sales promotion only	23	4	9	10
Advertising and sales promotion	13	3	4	6
Total	51	12	19	20

tially large, although informal, role. One advertising department did take a broader view of its functions in seeing itself as having "stewardship responsibility" for the divisions. It therefore evaluated all aspects of the divisions' advertising as well as that of competitors. However, even in this case it could not be said that the advertising specialist had a determining role in promotional budgeting. In most cases the advertising agency was likely to have a greater role in promotional planning than the advertising specialist.

The position of the functional specialist is likely to be considerably different in a company that does not use the product manager form of organization. In the one company of this type where interviews took place, the advertising and sales promotion departments were each charged with the responsibility for developing budgets for each brand. These were then presented to the marketing manager, who made the final decision.

Relationship with Sales Promotion

The influence of the sales promotion specialist was not mentioned by Robinson and Luck (1964), which suggests, as Kotler (1975) has noted, that this is a recently developed functional specialty. In fact, the appointment of sales promotion specialists has paralleled the growth of sales promotion as an element of brand strategy. The survey showed that respondents were more likely to have sales promotion specialists than advertising specialists and that, unlike advertising, more sales promotion specialists have been appointed since 1970 than in the preceding ten years (Table 5.4). Executives in the interviews also reported major efforts to upgrade these positions and to give the sales promotion specialist greater responsibility.

This does not mean, however, that they have any greater influence on the promotional budget decision than the advertising specialist. A review of Table 5.3 shows that, like advertising, more than half the departments are responsible for preparing proposals and that only 14 percent of the divisional specialists have an approval role. Similarly, the question on planning activities (Table 3.2) revealed that they were most likely to be responsible for the preparation of detailed plans and budgets rather than for the determination of promotional strategy. The executives who were interviewed described the role of the sales promotion specialist in similar terms to those used to discuss the advertising specialist with one exception: they were more involved with program execution. As one product manager commented, "Once the promotion plan is developed then we use the sales promotion department to help with the execution."

This greater role in execution appeared to reflect the unwillingness of many companies to fully utilize the services of sales promotion houses in the same way that they rely on advertising agencies. Executives who were interviewed in both the companies and the sales promotion organizations reported that these agencies were rarely involved in promotional planning. Further evidence of this is provided by respondents to the mail survey where only 18 companies indicated any involvement by a sales promotion agency in sales promotion planning and budgeting (Table 5.3).

Sales promotion specialists were strongly identified with program execution, and a number of departments had production facilities of their own. This appeared to be the traditional base upon which some sales promotion department had developed. However, this was apparently a much less important task for the more recently appointed sales promotion executives in the companies that were interviewed. Their main task was to help improve sales promotion programs by counseling the product managers.

The planning process described in the Vick Chemical Company case (Davis and Shapiro 1974) reflects the different roles of advertising and sales promotion specialists that were observed in several companies. In this case the product manager for Lavoris consulted with the advertising agency in preparing the advertising program for the brand and ignored the advertising specialist staff who provided what was primarily a media-buying service. However, for sales promotion planning, he worked with the sales promotion specialist on the corporate staff and not with an outside agency.

COORDINATION OF INFORMATION AND PLANNING

It is clear that the quality of promotional decisions is influenced by the type of information that is available and the extent to which it is used. This section examines the sources of information that were available to the product manager and the nature of the information that they provided, as well as the channels by which this information was made available and the extent to which it was used.

The product managers could draw on many sources in developing promotional strategy. These included marketing research, marketing planning, finance, outside agencies, and executives in the areas of sales, advertising, and sales promotion. The nature of the information that they could provide ranged from self-seeking opinions

TABLE 5.5

Research Budgets for Advertising and Sales Promotion
(in percent)

Question: "In the aggregate, about what percentage of sales for established brands would be budgeted for research in advertising and sales promotion?"

Percentage of Sales	Advertising	Sales Promotion
None	4	17
Less than 0.25 percent	25	46
0.25 to 1.00 percent	46	11
More than 1.00 percent	17	9
Not applicable/no response	9	18

Note: Figures may not total 100 because of rounding.

to experienced judgments to empirical research and models. Unfortunately, among the executives who were interviewed, the bulk of this information appeared to be from the opinion end of the spectrum.

The extent to which survey respondents were willing to provide formal research support for advertising and sales promotion decision making can be seen in Table 5.5. The table shows that 88 percent reportedly made some provision for advertising research, while 66 percent had budgeted amounts for sales promotion research. However, it is clear that more attention is paid to advertising research than to gathering information about sales promotion, both in terms of the percentage of sales budgeted for research and in the greater range of research measures employed. Table 5.6 shows that two-thirds of the measures suggested were more likely to be used to evaluate advertising than to test sales promotion. Table 5.7 indicates that respondent companies that did use formal quantitative models were more likely to use them for advertising planning than for sales promotion.

The company interviews suggested that relatively little of the research information that was gathered in either of these areas was

TABLE 5.6

Evaluation Measures

Question: "Which of these measures, if any, are normally used to evaluate advertising and sales promotion programs for major established brands?"

Measure	Percentage of Respondents	
	Advertising	Sales Promotion
No formal evaluation	5	14
Consumer awareness	89	12
Consumer attitudes	84	18
Consumer panel data	60	28
Sales volume (units)	72	74
Sales volume (dollars)	61	63
Market share	81	72
Distribution level	42	63
Profitability	65	51
Executive judgment	75	58
No response	2	4

TABLE 5.7

Use of Quantitative Models

Question: "Are formal quantitative models used to aid advertising and/or sales promotion decision making?"

	Percentage of Respondents
No quantitative models used	49
Models used for:	
Allocating total funds to advertising and sales promotion	23
Allocating funds to advertising	23
Allocating funds to sales promotion	11
Media planning and selection	40
No response	4

Note: Figures may not total 100 because of rounding.

designed to assist with the promotional allocation decision. Most of the research was likely to be concerned with evaluating the general sales performance of the brand and with improving the effectiveness of individual campaigns. It was, therefore, involved with sales and share analysis, copy testing, and evaluation of individual sales promotion activities. The relatively few attempts to evaluate the effectiveness of the promotional mix were discussed in the preceding chapter. They included the use of a syndicated market simulation model, the development of regression-based models, and several experimental studies.

In comparison with the findings of Robinson and Luck (1964), the companies in the present study appeared to have made some attempt to improve the channels by which this information is provided to the product manager. There was formal liaison with marketing research in all the companies that were interviewed (as was found in the earlier study), but there seemed to be major improvements in liaison with sales and finance. In regard to the sales department, several companies had established staff positions within the sales department, whose occupants were primarily concerned with liaison between sales and marketing management. With respect to promotional budgeting, their main role was likely to be in providing information regarding sales targets for the brand and in working on the development of sales promotion budgets, especially trade promotion. It was not possible to determine the extent to which this has helped promotional decision making, but it can be said to reflect a recognition by the sales department of the major role of marketing and a desire to improve relationships.

The interview study also revealed several examples of close liaison between product management and financial executives. In one company financial staff was attached to the product group and interacted with product managers daily to provide information on brand performance and the impact of proposed decisions and to help evaluate past promotional activities. In another company the financial staff was required to attend every brand planning meeting, to evaluate the profitability of proposed promotional strategies, and to liaise with marketing research and sales to check brand objectives and spending strategy. In both these companies there was a notable emphasis on profitability, as distinct from the volume orientation in several other cases.

Liaison with other groups within the companies that were interviewed and with advertising agencies did not appear to have a major effect on the promotional allocation decision. This largely reflects the finding, mentioned earlier, that these individuals are not likely to be involved in promotional planning until after the basic strategy has been determined.

Despite the improvement in the type of information that was available and in the channels by which it was provided, many of the limitations on its use that Robinson and Luck noted were found in this study. These included an apparent reluctance on the part of product managers to use information from past promotional activities in terms of their impact on profits.

A number of product managers who were interviewed appeared reluctant to use research on previous promotional programs, partly because they felt the findings did not apply to the situation they faced, partly because they, apparently, had confidence in their own problem-solving abilities, and in some cases because they were unaware that such information existed. One notable exception to this was the company that had collected the results of all its various sales promotion campaigns and summarized them as a guide for product managers as to what programs were likely to be most effective under what circumstances. The sales promotion department of one large advertising agency also provided this service to its clients.

One further reason for the failure to use data from previous promotional activities could be that formal evaluations, especially in terms of the impact on profits, were not always undertaken. This was most likely with advertising, where there was rarely an attempt to link a specific program to a particular response. There was more attention paid to program evaluation in sales promotion, but often this was no more than recording the number of cases that were sold during the period with no regard for the effect on profits or on postpromotional sales.

Several examples of the lack of awareness of the information that was available were also discovered in the interviews. All three companies that utilized the syndicated market structure model reported difficulty in persuading product managers to take advantage of its potential. In another company, a senior corporate planning executive had made an extensive analysis of the effects of promotional activities on the company's brands and had presented the results to the corporate officers and directors, but the product managers were unaware that this information was available.

It was not possible to test the Robinson and Luck hypothesis that the amount and usefulness of research depended on the extent of the research specialist's responsibilities and the budgeting procedure. However, it is possible to conclude with them that, despite the major steps that have been taken to improve the nature and availability of information, most decisions in promotional planning are still made on a largely intuitive basis.

6

IMPACT OF MARKETING STRATEGY
DECISIONS ON PROMOTIONAL PLANNING

Promotional planning and strategy are not only affected by organizational factors; they must also be developed in relation to the overall marketing strategy decided upon for the brand and the corporation as a whole. This chapter examines the impact on promotional strategy of such factors as relative importance of the brand, adoption of the system of strategic classification of brands (described earlier), and other marketing strategy options. The chapter discusses the question of strategic adaptation—the causes and direction of the changes that are made in promotional plans after they are implemented.

IMPORTANCE OF BRAND

Two earlier studies have found a relationship between the relative importance of a brand in terms of present or potential profitability or share of sales dollars and the extent to which it is supported by advertising. In his study Hurwood (1968) noted that "a number of companies report that the products which make the greatest contribution to overall profits are the ones favored in terms of all-out advertising support" (p. 11). Similarly, Marschner (1967) reported that both the oil company and the food-manufacturing company that he studied used profitability as a criterion for allocating advertising funds to regional markets. This procedure is intuitively rational since a company should provide strong support for those products that are most important to its current financial health. The one danger is that too much support may be given to products that have reached the mature stage in their life and not enough to products that are in the critical introductory phase.

TABLE 6.1

Impacts on Advertising/Sales Promotion Allocation:
Internal Factors
(in percent)

Question: "In your judgment which of the following factors do you
think would tend to increase the importance of advertising over
sales promotion, increase the importance of sales promotion over
advertising, or have neither effect on expenditures?"

Factor	Increase Advertising	Increase Sales Promotion	Neither	Number Responding
Brand has a contribution rate above division average	43	10	47	51
Brand has a contribution rate above corporate average	35	6	59	49
Brand sells at a higher price than competing national brands	68	16	16	50
Consumers report the brand to be of higher quality than competing national brands	78	2	20	49

Several executives in the interview phase of the study mentioned
that the profit margin on a brand would influence the promotional mix.
This influence is at least partly derived from the fact that, since the
advertising and sales promotion budget is determined as a residual
from sales, profits, and costs, the larger the profit margin, the
greater the total budget is likely to be. As was mentioned in Chapter
4, several executives reported that the larger the total budget, the
more likely it was that advertising would receive a major allocation.
In fact, this pattern was specifically suggested for brands with high
profit margins.

This question was addressed to the respondents in the mail
survey, and their answers are summarized in Table 6.1. These ex-

ecutives are divided as to whether brand profit margins affect the promotional mix, but those who feel that there is some impact clearly
support the importance of advertising for brands with above-average
margins.

STRATEGIC CLASSIFICATION

The widespread use of the product portfolio concept and its effects on the allocation decision process were discussed in Chapter 4.
This section examines the effect of such a classification system on
the promotional strategy for a company's brands based on the practices of the two companies in the interview study that had adopted such
a system.

In the original formulation of the product portfolio concept,
products were classified into four groups on the basis of their market
share and perceived growth potential. These groups were: high
growth/low share ("question mark"), high growth/high share ("star"),
low growth/high share ("cash cow"), and low growth/low share ("pet")
(Boston Consulting Group 1970).

As mentioned in the earlier discussion, the Boston Consulting
Group (BCG) recommends differing strategies for each brand, depending on the group into which it is classified. "Question marks"
and "stars" should be supported heavily to ensure that the maximum
growth potential is obtained. "Cash cows" should be supported only
at the lowest level required to ensure maximum cash flow. "Pets"
should not be supported at all and should be liquidated as soon as possible.

In both the companies that used this system, the initial classification into strategic categories was made by a top-level marketing
committee that included both corporate and division executives. A
detailed examination of the history, present position, and future potential of each brand was made, and the brands were divided into the
appropriate groups. One of the companies used a threefold classification system:

Group I included brands that had sales growth of more than 15
percent per annum and that were at least holding market share. They
were also required to be in markets that were expanding by more than
5 percent each year.

Group II included brands that appeared to have a large, stable
market share and that offered a good profit margin. Most of the
company's brands were in this category.

Group III brands were those that were slowly losing sales and
that had modest profit margins.

The effects on promotional strategy were as follows:

Group I: For these brands the level and mix of sales promotion could vary from year to year according to perceived needs. The planners had three broad options: (1) to maintain the same level of spending (in all groups past history was important in determining the spending levels, which were not the same for all brands in a group); (2) to increase total spending; this would be implemented by increasing advertising spending and maintaining sales promotion at the same rate; and (3) to cut the price and maintain advertising and sales promotion spending rates; this would reduce the brand contribution rate, but it would allow it to capture a larger share of the market, which would provide a larger base to draw on when the brand became a "cash cow."

Group II: These brands were considerably more restricted and were held to the same level of advertising and sales promotion spending each year. In theory the only variation came from the fact that advertising spending was defined as an absolute amount, which may or may not be adjusted for inflation from year to year. On the other hand, sales promotion spending was on a per-case basis. This meant that over time sales promotion usually became an even more important element of the promotional mix.

Group III: These brands were generally denied any advertising support, but sales promotion spending was maintained on a per-case rate. Most of this sales promotion activity was directed to the trade to maintain distribution.

TABLE 6.2

Effect of Strategic Classification on Promotional Allocations
(marketer of personal-care products)

Category	Total Budget (as a percentage of sales)	Advertising	Sales Promotion
Question mark	Highest	High	Moderate*
Star	High	High	Low
Cash cow	Moderate	Low	Moderate
Pet	Lowest	None	High

*May be high if required by introductory strategy.

The other company that used the product portfolio concept used the same groups that the BCG had defined. Once again, the actual spending levels differed from brand to brand, but the effect on promotional strategy was similar in each group. These effects are summarized in Table 6.2. The general pattern is similar to that already described.

OTHER STRATEGIC CHOICES

Push Strategy versus a Pull Strategy

Brands that are "pushed" through the distribution channel with the support of heavy trade incentives are likely to have a different promotional mix than brands that rely on advertising and consumer promotions to create demand "pull." The executives who were interviewed rarely discussed these as distinct strategic options, perhaps because the study focused on established brands where the basic strategy was already determined and where promotional activities were directed to both groups. In most cases the issue was the relative degree of emphasis to be placed on securing trade support versus promoting directly to the consumer. The only occasions when there was a clear switch in emphasis was when advertising support was withdrawn from a brand perceived as having a limited future market.

Premium Brand versus Price Brand

In the interview study several executives mentioned the privileged position of a brand that was successfully positioned as a premium entry in a market. It was suggested that this brand could ignore sales promotion-oriented competitors and, indeed, that it would be detrimental to its position to indulge in this type of activity. Two characteristics of a premium brand are its higher price and its perceived higher quality. Questions on the effect of each of these conditions were included in the survey questionnaire. Respondents' answers are shown in Table 6.1. They clearly indicate the opinion that brands that sell at higher prices and that are of a higher perceived quality are more likely to rely on advertising than sales promotion in their promotional mix.

Related to the premium brand strategy is the option of a price brand that competes at the bottom end of the market. One application of this strategy is to introduce a new brand or to convert an established brand to a low-price, promotion-oriented strategy. This brand receives little or no advertising support but will often have a substantial sales promotion program directed both to the trade and the consumer. This may be used as a response to a new competitor—especially a lower-priced competitor—and may serve to protect the company's premium brand from direct competition.

STRATEGIC RESPONSES: PROGRAM ADAPTATION

In the discussion of the promotional planning process (Chapter 3), it was recognized that the majority of respondent companies changed their promotional allocations after they had been established in the annual plan. Not only did they change programs but these changes were of a size and frequency to have a significant effect on promotional strategy (see Table 3.3). This section seeks to identify the factors that are most important in causing companies to change their advertising and sales promotion budgets and to describe the impact of these changes on promotional strategy.

In the company interview phase of the study, it was found that the two most widely mentioned reasons for changing the advertising and sales promotion budgets were, first, a failure to meet plan goals and, second, the need to respond to competitors. Therefore, a series of questions was included in the mail questionnaire that sought execu-

TABLE 6.3

Impacts on Advertising/Sales Promotion Decision:
Performance Factors
(in percent)

Factor	Increase Advertising	Increase Sales Promotion	Neither	Number Responding
Brand is not meeting sales targets	10	61	29	51
Brand is not meeting profit targets	12	35	53	51
Brand is ahead of sales targets	42	8	50	50
Brand is in a product category that is ahead of profit targets	44	4	52	50

tives' opinions regarding the impact on the promotional mix of both of these conditions.

In regard to the first situation, Table 6.3 shows that 61 percent of the respondents perceived a failure to meet sales goals as being met by an increased allocation to sales promotion, while 35 percent favored this action for a brand that was not meeting profit goals. Brands that were ahead of sales or profit goals were thought likely to receive increased advertising support from slightly more than 40 percent of the respondents, but about 50 percent expressed the opinion that there would be no change in the promotional mix. Respondents' views on the effects of competitors' strategies are presented in Table 7.3, where about half indicated that they would expect to see a change in allocation to advertising or sales promotion to match the particular strategy adopted by the competitor.

To obtain a more detailed perspective on the factors that initiated change and their impact on the elements of the promotional mix, respondents were asked to indicate the direction of their budget changes for established brands during the previous fiscal year and the reasons for these changes. Table 6.4 relates the direction of the changes to the four most frequently mentioned reasons for these modifications. Many respondents gave multiple responses and more than one reason; so there is some overlap. To reduct this overlap, the response "both directions during the year" has been eliminated. This reduces the number of responses, but in most cases the impact of each factor is clear.

The most frequently reported reason for changes in the advertising or sales promotion budget was a failure to meet profit objectives. This was not unexpected given the frequency with which it was mentioned in the interviews and the earlier discussion of the importance of financial goals in both the initial planning process and the reviews. It appears that the primary response to this situation is to cut spending, particularly the total advertising and sales promotion budget and expenditures on advertising. This pattern of reducing expenditures to meet profit goals was reported by many executives in the interviews and appears to be common in the industry. One executive described the attitude in his company: "We don't have a budget that is not attainable—sales may be down but not profits." A similar procedure is reported for the General Foods orange drink, Tang, where planned advertising was cut by one-third and sales promotion expenditures were increased to meet the financial goals for 1973 (Singer and DeBruicker 1975a). This pattern explains why many respondents saw failure to meet goals as not increasing the importance of either advertising or sales promotion—the primary reaction is to cut expenditures on both.

Changes in response to competitive activity were the next most commonly mentioned in the survey. In this situation the impact was

TABLE 6.4

Reasons for Budget Changes
(number of times mentioned)

Question: "What were the two or three most common reasons for these changes?"

Reason	Total Budget		Advertising Budget		Consumer Promotion Budget		Trade Promotion Budget	
	Increase	Decrease	Increase	Decrease	Increase	Decrease	Increase	Decrease
Profits below expectations	1	9	3	10	3	4	6	3
Competitors' strategy	4	0	5	1	3	3	3	1
Sales below expectations	1	4	1	6	1	1	2	3
Sales above expectations	4	0	3	1	3	0	3	0

generally to increase the total budget as well as advertising and trade promotion expenditures. This action was reported by several executives in the interviews and reflects a concern to maintain relative levels of promotional activity. Analyses developed by the A. C. Nielsen Company (Peckham 1973) have suggested that it is important for brands to maintain their share of both advertising and consumer-oriented sales promotion expenditures, and this view may influence these managers. In fact, this pattern of matching competitors' actions has been noted throughout the study.

The final group of factors relates to performance above or below sales targets. As might be anticipated from the earlier discussion, the responses are in opposite directions. Where sales goals are not met, there appeared to be an effort to reduce expenditures, especially for advertising. Where sales are higher than expected, expenditures were increased in all areas.

These were the only reasons for budget changes mentioned by more than three respondents. Other factors that were reported related to the use of test market results, decisions to introduce a new product, changes in timing of promotional programs, and changes in product goals as a reason for changing the budget. In the interview study it was found that, as has been discussed above, there was considerable pressure to deliver the "bottom line." This meant that budgets were changed, but goals were rarely revised, particularly financial goals. This suggests a lack of understanding of (or an unwillingness to recognize) the relationship between promotional strategy and brand performance. It also leads to inefficient and possibly detrimental tactics such as "buying" sales from future periods with increased trade promotion activity.

7
IMPACT OF EXTERNAL FACTORS
ON PROMOTIONAL STRATEGY

In the initial discussion of promotional strategy, it was noted that it was determined "partly independently and partly in response to changing environmental conditions." This chapter draws on the findings of the interview study and the responses to the mail survey to identify the specific factors in the environment that executives report as influencing the promotional allocation decision and to evaluate the nature of their impact.

Four groups of potentially influential factors were identified from the literature and the interviews. These groups include market factors, competitive factors, consumer factors, and distribution factors.

MARKET FACTORS

Brand Life Cycle

One of the most widely used conceptual frameworks in marketing is the product or brand life cycle. As the sales and profit pattern of the brand changes over time, so marketing strategy must change in order to maintain a viable business. Not only are different marketing strategies appropriate at different stages but promotional strategies should also change. Although no empirical evidence is presented, Kotler (1972) suggests that the relationship between advertising and sales promotion may change as follows:

Introduction: Advertising and sales promotion are equally important—the former to make potential customers aware of the product, while the latter "facilitates interest and trial."

Growth: Advertising is assumed to be much more important than sales promotion.

Maturity: Sales promotion becomes increasingly important. "In the mature stage of many processed food products, deal expentures may account for as much as 50 percent of total expenditures on advertising and dealing."

Decline: Sales promotion is much more important than advertising (pp. 659-60).

The importance of the brand life cycle was reinforced by the executives who were interviewed with most of them indicating that it was a major influence on their decisions as to the appropriate promotional mix. The respondents' general view of the most appropriate strategy in each of the stages was as follows:

Introduction: Advertising and sales promotion are equally important for the introductory period, which usually lasts less than one year. Some products may have unique qualities that are best expressed through advertising, but "me-too" products are more likely to rely on consumer promotion. For most consumer nondurable goods, heavy trade promotion is required to secure distribution.

Growth: Advertising is more important than sales promotion as companies seek to increase awareness of their brand.

Maturity: Sales promotion is increasingly important. An important determining factor is the degree of customer loyalty obtained. If loyalty is high, then advertising is still dominant. If loyalty is low, then sales promotion is increasingly important and may take the larger share of the budget in later years.

Decline: Advertising is of little importance and will be dropped entirely in most cases. Sales promotion is generally directed to the trade to maintain distribution.

An example of the effect of the brand life cycle on the advertising/sales promotion allocation decision is provided in Table 7.1. The data for the six brands of household nonfood products show that both the total budget and the allocation are different at different stages in the cycle. This company is somewhat unusual in having such a high ratio of advertising to sales promotion in the late-maturity stage of the brand's life cycle, a situation that probably results from the company's dominant position in this market. The effects of market dominance will be discussed in the next section.

Further evidence of the pattern is provided in Pfizer's Hai Karate line of men's fragrances (Ryan and Scott 1977). Here the proportion of the total advertising and sales promotion budget allocated to advertising was 57 percent in the introductory year, rose to 67 percent in the next year, and steadily declined thereafter until it

TABLE 7.1

Impacts of Life Cycle on Allocation Decision
(manufacturer of household nonfood products)

Stage in Life Cycle	Brand	Percentage of Sales Spent on Advertising and Sales Promotion	Advertising as a Percentage of Total Advertising and Sales Promotion
Introduction	A	32	50
Growth	B	31	61
Maturity	C	22	82
	D	16	81
Decline	E	16	19
	F	8	0

Source: Company records.

was only 48 percent in the fifth year after a launch. A similar pattern is seen in the allocation patterns for the brands discussed in Table 4.3. In all cases the trend is for advertising to decrease in importance over time.

Because of the importance of this factor, respondents to the questionnaire were asked to evaluate the effect of the different life cycle stages on the relative importance of advertising and sales promotion. Their answers are presented in Table 7.2. This demonstrates that respondents clearly perceive advertising to be more important in the growth stage and, to a lesser extent, in the introductory stage of the cycle. Sales promotion is thought to be more important in the maturity and decline stages. There is some support for sales promotion in the introduction of a product and for advertising during the maturity stage, but the majority opinion is unmistakable. The views expressed in the literature were therefore supported by the respondents in this study.

This pattern of advertising/sales promotion spending is likely to be interrupted where there is a major relaunch or repositioning of a brand. Executives commented that relaunch was likely to be accompanied by greatly increased investments in advertising as well as some sales promotion. If the repositioning is successful, the prod-

TABLE 7.2

Impacts on Promotional Strategy: Market Factors
(in percent)

Question: "In your judgment which of the following factors do you
think would tend to increase the importance of advertising over
sales promotion, increase the importance of sales promotion
over advertising, or have no effect?"

Factor	Increase Advertising	Increase Sales Promotion	Neither	Number Responding
Life cycle: brand is at				
Introductory stage	59	31	10	51
Growth stage	75	15	10	52
Mature stage	24	50	26	50
Decline stage	8	76	16	51
Brand has highly seasonal sales (more than 40 percent sales in one quarter)	27	33	39	51
Brand is sold only in limited geographic regions	4	29	67	51

Note: Figures may not total 100 because of rounding.

uct is likely to repeat at least the growth stage of the life cycle with
consequent changes in advertising and sales promotion allocations.

Seasonality

The impact of seasonality may be seen as a special application
of the same pattern observed in the brand life cycle. This is due to
the fact that seasonal products have to be relaunched every year.
Executives who were interviewed reported that this usually required
additional expenditures on trade allowances and consumer promotion
to ensure that retailers stocked the product prior to the selling season.

This was said to be a particular problem for products such as soft drinks, which are likely to lose a considerable proportion of their shelf facings during the winter months. The overall result was that sales promotion was expected to be a more important part of the promotional mix than for other products at similar stages in their life cycle. Respondents to the survey did not express a clear opinion on this factor. There was a marginal preference for sales promotion, but the largest group (39 percent) decided that it would have no effect either way (Table 7.2).

Limited Geographic Area

During the interviews it was suggested that brands that were sold only in limited or regional markets were likely to be forced to allocate relatively more of their funds to sales promotion than similar national brands. Two reasons were proposed. First, regional brands were seen as having less bargaining power than national brands with large retail chains, and second, because they were forced to pay higher rates for television time, regional companies could not afford to match the strategy of their larger competitors.

Table 7.2 shows that, while most respondents felt that this had no effect on the relative importance of either sales promotion or advertising, those who did perceive an effect (33 percent) were strongly in favor of increased sales promotion. The size of the group that reported no effect may be due to lack of direct experience by many of the respondents who were generally associated with large firms and national brands.

General Economic Conditions

In his study of marketing planning, Hurwood (1968) found that companies were likely to reduce spending on advertising when economic conditions were unfavorable and to increase expenditures as conditions improved. On the other hand, several executives who were interviewed suggested that one of the reasons for the rapid growth in sales promotion expenditures was the difficult economic conditions of the 1973-75 period. On this basis it could be expected that the allocation decision would be affected by the economic environment.

Several of these executives reported this as a factor in their allocation decision. The problem appeared to be most acute for marketers of products that were not seen as essential by the consumer and that met considerable sales resistance in the face of inflation-induced price increases. In this situation one marketer of household cleaning products was forced to increase sales promotion expenditures substantially to maintain volume. Another product manager noted an increased response to a competitor's sales promotion activity during this period and was forced to modify allocations accordingly. Support for this strategy comes from the Target Group Index (Axiom Market Research Bureau 1974) and other studies that show an increase in coupon usage during the 1973–75 recession and again in the high-inflation periods of the late 1970s.

COMPETITIVE FACTORS

Market Share

While earlier discussion indicated that important brands were more likely to receive promotional support, several studies, particularly those with the PIMS data base, have shown that a larger market share was associated with relatively lower levels of total promotional spending (Buzzell, Gale, and Sultan 1974). Several factors could account for this. A larger volume of sales might mean that a brand could be supported by the same or a greater amount of advertising dollars than a competitor's but at a lower unit rate. Another reason could be the greater bargaining power of a large brand, which would allow it to spend proportionally less on allowances to secure trade support. Some evidence for this is provided by a Booz, Allen & Hamilton study (1974) of grocery dealing, which found that expected brand volume was the second most important reason for a retailer's decision to support a trade deal.

Both of these reasons were reported by executives in the interviews, but they suggested that, while the total budget for advertising and sales promotion might be lower, there would also be differences in the way the funds were allocated. One executive noted that in a market that one of his company's brands dominated it was well able to maintain an allocation of 60 percent or more to advertising but that in a market in which it was the second largest brand it had to allocate more than 50 percent of its funds to sales promotion. A similar situation is reported for Regular Maxwell House Coffee (Marshall 1975), which has the largest share of the national market for regular coffee and is the dominant brand in the eastern half of the country. In 1968 its overall allocation was 50 percent advertising and 50 percent sales promotion. However, in many western markets the brand had only the third largest market share, and, not only was the company forced to spend at a higher per-case rate in these markets but also its allocation favored sales promotion with only 40 percent of the funds going to advertising.

TABLE 7.3

Impacts on Promotional Strategy: Competitive Factors
(in percent)

Factor	Increase Advertising	Increase Sales Promotion	Neither	Number Responding
The brand				
Has the largest share of any brand in its market	57	12	31	49
Has one or more competitors with similar market shares	46	36	18	50
Is facing a major competing brand that				
Cut advertising and increased sales promotion	17	48	35	48
Increased advertising and cut sales promotion	51	10	39	49
Is in a market where private labels have more than 25 percent of total sales volume	45	30	26	47
Is considered to be well differentiated from competing national brands	78	4	18	50

Note: Figures may not total 100 because of rounding.

This view was supported by respondents to the survey with 57 percent of them expressing the opinion that a brand that had the largest share of its market would be more likely to rely on advertising than sales promotion in its promotional strategy (see Table 7.3).

A different allocation decision was expected in the competitive situation where no one brand dominates a market but where two or more brands have relatively equal shares. Executives who were interviewed suggested that this condition would tend to increase the importance of sales promotion, because, under these circumstances, no one brand would have economies of scale nor an advantage in dealing with the trade. One corporate executive noted that in this situation the trade often tried to play competing manufacturers against each other to increase the allowances provided.

In the survey the largest number of respondents (46 percent) perceived advertising to be the more important, but a sizable group (36 percent) supported the role of sales promotion (Table 7.3). This could suggest that the particular strategy adopted by competitors is more important to the allocation decision than to the market structure, which may be a reason why some markets require heavy sales promotion spending (for example, coffee) while others rely more on advertising (for example, breakfast cereals). The president of Alberto-Culver has noted this effect on advertising levels in commenting that his company's "deodorant maintenance advertising budget is greater than the hair spray maintenance advertising budget because deodorant manufacturers advertise heavily whereas hair spray manufacturers do not" (Clarke and Marshall 1973).

Competitive Strategy

The importance of monitoring competitors' expenditures and adapting strategy to meet their efforts has been mentioned in the literature and discussed earlier in relation to methods of allocating the promotional budget.

In the survey respondents were asked to give their opinions of the effect on the allocation decision of two contrasting changes in strategy by a major competing brand. Their answers in Table 7.3 indicate that they saw the appropriate response as being to match the competitor's strategy by increasing advertising (51 percent of respondents) or sales promotion (48 percent of respondents). It is interesting to note that slightly more than one-third of the respondents felt that the changes in competitors' strategies would have no effect.

A finding such as this illustrates a problem that several executives in the interview study found difficult to solve—the problem of determining the most appropriate response to competitors, particularly an aggressive new entrant in the market or an established competitor who embarked on a heavily sales promotion-oriented campaign. Most of the executives were of the same opinion as the survey respondents, namely, that a substantial increase in sales promotion activity was the best defense in the short term at least. However, there are some dangers in this approach, and these will be discussed in the last chapter.

Private-Label Competition

Several executives who were interviewed indicated that the strength of private-label competitors influenced their advertising/ sales promotion allocation decision. Their view was that the larger the share of the market held by private labels, the greater the proportion of funds that had to be allocated to sales promotion. This reflected their perceptions of the greater importance of price in consumers' decision making in these markets and the need for marketers of nationally advertised brands to use sales promotion to reduce the price differential.

In the mail survey respondents were asked their opinion of the effects on promotional allocations of having a brand in a market where private labels had more than 25 percent of total sales volume (this is approximately twice the average share of the market for private labels of consumer nondurable goods). As Table 7.3 shows, the largest group of respondents (45 percent) favored an increase in advertising, possibly to counter the price advantage by stressing product benefits. A smaller group (30 percent) did support sales promotion efforts, but the responses indicate some division of opinion on this factor.

Degree of Differentiation

Several executives who were interviewed mentioned that a brand that was highly differentiated from its competitors' would be more likely to have a promotional strategy that favored advertising. One reason for this was that with a differentiated product there were usually more features or benefits to be communicated to the prospective customer. Another reason was the belief that advertising was likely to be more effective for differentiated products than for basic commodities.

This was found to be a difficult concept to operationalize; so in the survey the question was simply asked in relation to a brand that was "considered to be well differentiated from competing national brands." The responses in Table 7.3 indicate that a substantial majority of the respondents (78 percent) support the view that advertising is more important than sales promotion in the promotional strategy for a highly differentiated brand. This should also be related to the responses to questions about specific dimensions on which a brand might be differentiated—that is, higher prices and higher quality. The responses to these questions were discussed in the preceding chapter and were presented in Table 6.1. They indicated similarly strong support for the importance of advertising under these conditions.

CONSUMER FACTORS

Although no consumer factors have been specifically identified in the literature as affecting the advertising/sales promotion mix for a brand, it is obvious that they have a strong influence. For example, sales promotion activities are important in the introductory stage of the brand life cycle to encourage consumer trial. Advertising is likely to remain an important element in the introductory, growth, and early-maturity phases of the life cycle, initially to make consumers aware of the product and later to communicate differentiating features.

During the personal interviews, executives suggested several consumer-related factors that could explain differences in advertising/sales promotion strategy. These could be classified into two groups: factors relating to the decision process (degree of loyalty, degree of perceived risk) and the characteristics of the consumer (age, income level).

Consumer-Decision Process

Many of the executives interviewed in the study expressed the belief that advertising was more important than sales promotion for a brand with highly loyal customers. This was partly founded on the view that for these brands sales promotion would be little more than a reward for customers who would have purchased the brand anyway. The one exception to this was when executives felt that there was a chance to attract new customers to a brand. Thus, the marketer of a personal hygiene product with highly loyal customers employed a heavy sampling program at regular intervals to encourage new entrants to the market to adopt the brand. The corollary to this view was put forward by some managers who saw little value in advertising in a market where there was little brand loyalty and a good deal of brand switching. The issue of loyalty was not addressed in the survey, but high loyalty is likely to be closely related to high differentiation (since loyal customers presumably see their brand as significantly different from competitors'). The responses to this question, as noted earlier, support the importance of advertising.

Several executives who were interviewed mentioned that advertising was likely to be an important element in promotional strategy for products with a high degree of perceived risk associated with their purchase. The basis for this conclusion was the view that in situations of high risk consumers would be more willing to look for information and would thus be more interested in advertising. Perceived risk is not likely to be a factor in the purchase of many consumer nondurable goods because they are usually low priced and readily evaluated and involve little personal or social commitment. However, it was thought that the concept might operate in cases where the product was purchased at infrequent intervals so that consumers would have less experiential knowledge. Respondents in the survey were therefore asked to indicate their opinions as to the influence of frequency of purchase on the promotional mix. As can be seen in Table 7.4, 41 percent of the respondents felt that a purchase frequency of

TABLE 7.4

Impacts on Advertising/Sales Promotion Decisions: Distribution and Consumer Factors
(in percent)

Factor	Increase Advertising	Increase Sales Promotion	Neither	Number Responding
The brand				
Is in danger of losing national distribution	15	71	15	48
Is purchased by consumer typically once every month or more frequently	51	8	41	49

Note: Figures may not total 100 because of rounding.

at least once a month would have no effect, but half the respondents (51 percent) perceived this as increasing the importance of advertising over sales promotion.

The answer to this apparent conflict has been suggested by Buzzell et al. (1972) and supported with empirical evidence in later work with Farris (Buzzell and Farris 1976). Their conclusion is that, up to the point where the consumer relies entirely on use behavior as a basis for decision making, the more frequently a consumer is in the market, the greater are the opportunities to influence choice. Many of the respondents appear to agree.

Consumer Characteristics

Several managers in the interview study indicated that certain consumer characteristics might influence the allocation decision. One of these characteristics was the age of the target customer; it was believed that brands aimed at children would be likely to rely more on sales promotion than brands of similar products direct to adults, since children are seen as having a low level of loyalty for many products. Executives from two companies provided specific examples of the effect of this factor on their promotional allocations. In the case of a food product, 70 percent of the total went to advertising for an adult-oriented brand and only 50 percent for a brand directed to children. For a personal-care item, 60 percent of the budget was in advertising for the adult version and only 47 percent for the child-oriented brand.

It was also suggested that income level might be an influencing factor in view of the fact that one of the most widely employed sales promotion devices, coupons, is more likely to be used by middle-income households than by other groups (Axiom Market Research Bureau 1974). However, no specific examples of this were provided.

DISTRIBUTION FACTORS

Pressure from distributors generally takes the form of demands for increased allowances and other promotional support as a prerequisite for stocking or promoting the brand. This is not specifically addressed in the literature, although the impact is mentioned in relation to the brand life cycle, where a high degree of sales promotion activity is required to get the product on the shelves in the introductory stage and to keep it stocked in the decline. This suggests that trade promotion activities are likely to be proportionately greater when the brand has a relatively weak sales pattern.

The increasing sophistication and power of mass retailers was also proposed as a reason for the increasing expenditures on sales promotion in recent years. One example of the impact of these trends was mentioned by several executives in the interview study. They commented that supermarket chains were more likely to request sales promotion support and were better organized to manage these activities than were drug chains. Thus, the level of sales promotion activity would be higher for the same brand sold through supermarkets than through drugstores.

The extent to which trade pressure influences brand promotional strategy is related to other factors that have been discussed above. Two of these were mentioned by one senior sales executive in noting that trade pressure was easier to resist, first, when a brand had a large market share and, second, when it was highly differentiated. He commented on the latter factor in relation to a highly successful brand that was unique at the time it was introduced and that established a new product category. The brand was now facing increased pressure because the trade saw it as a commodity. Executives also recognized that brands that were used as "loss leaders" (for example, coffee, mouthwash) were particularly likely to face trade pressure. In a general comment on the increased demands for allowances, one executive concluded, "It's like dope; they need a fix every three months."

In an attempt to measure the effects of the power of retailers, respondents to the mail survey were asked to indicate the impact on a brand's promotional strategy of the likely loss of national distribution. The answers in Table 7.4 show that most (71 percent) were of the opinion that in this situation sales promotion would be more important that advertising.

PRINCIPAL EXTERNAL DETERMINANTS
OF PROMOTIONAL STRATEGY

A number of factors have been identified that executives believed would influence decisions on the relative importance of advertising or sales promotion in established brands. The most important of these are summarized in Table 7.5. Many of these factors overlap, and they may be highly correlated. It is also important to recognize that in most cases a particular allocation decision will reflect the impact of a number of the factors described above. In some cases these may operate in the same direction—for example, a highly differentiated brand in the growth stage of the life cycle that dominates its market. In other cases there may be conflicts, as when a growth brand faces a promotion-oriented competitor. Therefore, the determination of

TABLE 7.5

Major Determinants of the Allocation Decision: External

	Impact on Allocation	
Factor	Increase Advertising	Increase Sales Promotion
Stage in brand life cycle		
Introduction	X	
Growth	X	
Maturity		X
Decline		X
Regional brand		X
Market dominance	X	
Promotion-oriented competitor		X
Advertising-oriented competitor	X	
High differentiation	X	
High purchase frequency	X	
Distribution vulnerability		X

which factors are likely to be most influential will require statistical analysis. This and other issues will be discussed in the concluding chapter.

8
PRINCIPLE FINDINGS AND CONCLUSIONS

This chapter presents a summary of the principal findings of the study as they relate to the promotional planning process, the allocation decision models, and the organizational, strategic, and environmental factors that influence promotional strategy. The second part of the chapter identifies a number of obstacles to effective promotional planning and suggests some corrective measures. The need for further research and conceptual development is examined in the final section.

SUMMARY OF PRINCIPAL FINDINGS

The Planning Process

The promotional budgeting process for established brands of consumer nondurable goods was found to be similar to the Adaptive Planning and Control Sequence (APACS) model only in a general way. The major differences between the two appeared to be, first, the increased involvement of senior management and, second, the use of planning procedures that appeared less effective than those proposed in the APACS formulation.

The increased involvement of senior management was likely to be reflected in the greater number of guidelines that were established (compared with the APACS schema) and by requirements for interim approvals of budgets. Among the suboptimal planning procedures was an apparent failure to consider alternative promotional mixes, a frequent reliance on what had been done in the past, and various constraints on decision makers and their use of information. The specific differences between the APACS model and the observed process were presented in Table 3.5.

It was proposed that a more useful description of the planning process as observed in the company interviews would recognize three planning stages, each separated by an approval step and followed by a review phase and adaption if required. The three planning phases were described as target planning (setting sales and financial targets for the brand), strategic planning (developing the preliminary budget including allocation), and tactical planning (preparation of detailed plans and budgets). This description was outlined in Figure 3.2.

The total budget for advertising and sales promotion was found to be determined as a residual from sales after the desired costs and profit had been provided for. Several authors in this field had reported similar conclusions.

Advertising/Sales Promotion Allocation Decision Models

The most frequently observed procedure for allocating funds between advertising and sales promotion was the use of a predetermined ratio. However, this was rarely found in the expected form of specific guidelines as to the relationship between advertising and sales promotion. The most common procedure was budgeting by precedent in the form of accepting the allocation for the preceding year. This resulted in a pattern of relatively similar allocations for a brand over a period of several years and then a major shift, followed by several years of stability. Another special case was the practice of classifying brands into strategic categories for which promotional spending had been established.

Other decision models included the buildup of budgets based on the most fixed element (usually trade promotion) with consumer promotion and advertising programs being added until the total budget was exhausted. Another approach was to attempt to match the allocation of one or more principal competitors. The practice of establishing objectives and then looking for the allocation that was likely to achieve them at minimum cost was also observed. These models were rarely found to be the primary basis for allocation and were most frequently observed in combination with other methods.

And, finally, the general preference among planners interviewed appeared to be the maintenance of a stable allocation pattern. This was demonstrated in a flow model of the allocation decision (see Figure 4.1).

Organizational Factors

The organizational factors that impacted upon promotional strategy decisions were found to include the position of the decision maker(s), the degree of decision freedom enjoyed by this individual, and the nature and extent of the information used to aid decision making. The major impact of these factors appeared to be in limiting the strategic options that the promotional planner could employ.

It was also found that generally the product manager did not have the ultimate (or, in many cases, even the major) responsibility for the advertising and sales promotion allocation decision for a brand. The product manager's role is restricted by executives at higher levels who set the total advertising and sales promotion budget for the brand, establish formal and informal guidelines, require approvals during and after the planning process, restrict certain promotional techniques, and determine the strategic category for the brand. On the other hand, product managers are likely to have the strongest influence on the allocation decision owing to their role as the prime initiator of strategies for the brand, their ability to negotiate changes in guidelines, and their major involvement in the preparation of preliminary budgets and in the establishment of advertising and sales promotion objectives as well as the development and coordination of plans and budgets in both these areas.

The allocation decision is also affected by the relationship between the product manager and the various functional specialists. Sales management appeared to be the only functional specialists that had any influence on the actual budget, but this appeared to be primarily through their ability to appeal directly to top management and to secure additional funds for brands that were facing strong competition. They also had some degree of influence in negotiating the proportion of the budget that would be allocated to trade promotion. Several examples were presented of efforts to give sales management greater freedom in their use of trade promotion funds under strong guidelines from product management.

Advertising and sales promotion specialists seemed to have little influence on the budget and were likely to be primarily involved in program execution. More surveyed companies had sales promotion specialists than had advertising specialists, and the former were more likely to have been appointed in the past seven years. Advertising agencies were likely to be heavily involved in developing programs for advertising, but there was little use of sales promotion agencies in this role. In this area product managers appeared to rely more on their company's own sales promotion specialists.

In addition, there seemed to be more information being gathered to aid the decision maker than was reported by Robinson and Luck (1964). However, most of this information was likely to be oriented to monitoring brand progress and not to evaluating promotional programs. Respondents spent proportionately more on advertising research than on sales promotion research for established brands.

Product managers did not appear to use all the information that was available to them and sometimes were not aware of other decision aids.

Impact of Marketing Strategy Decisions on Promotional Plans

In terms of strategies that were selected, respondents felt that the more profitable a brand was, the greater was the role of advertising in its promotional mix. A premium brand was also found to rely more on advertising than on sales promotion. Almost half the survey respondents reported that they had adopted the concept of classifying brands into groups for different strategic treatments. In these instances brands with high perceived growth potential were likely to have an allocation weighted to advertising, while those with a low-growth potential would rely more on sales promotion.

A majority of respondents reported that their advertising and sales promotion budgets were changed by more than 10 percent during the previous year. The two most frequently mentioned reasons for changes were a failure to meet plan goals and change as a response to a competitor's strategy. If the brand was failing to meet profit objectives, then the budget was likely to be cut, with most of the reduction coming from advertising. On the other hand, advertising was likely to be increased if the brand was exceeding its goals. Competitive activity was usually met with an increase in total promotional spending, particularly on advertising and trade promotion.

External Factors Influencing Promotional Strategy

A number of factors in the firm's environment were reported by executives as being likely to influence the advertising and sales promotion allocation decision. These were divided into four groups relating to the market, competition, consumers, and distribution. It was found that many of these factors overlapped and that they were highly correlated.

In regard to market factors, the most important appeared to be the stage in the product life cycle. Respondents were of the opinion that advertising would be more important in the introductory and growth stages, while sales promotion would be more important during maturity and decline. Several executives reported that they would spend more on sales promotion in the face of difficult economic conditions.

In terms of competition-related factors, respondents expected that a brand that dominated its market would allocate a greater pro-

portion of funds to advertising. Similar support would be given to a
brand that was perceived as highly differentiated from its competitors.
The particular advertising/sales promotion strategy that a competitor
adopted was also seen as influential with many executives, suggesting
that a company would try to match competitors' efforts.

Consumer-related factors included the degree of loyalty that
customers had to a brand, the frequency of purchase of the brand,
and whether the brand was purchased by or for children. Brands with
highly loyal customers and brands that were purchased monthly or
more frequently were perceived by executives as being more likely to
rely on advertising in their promotional mix. Brands that were directed toward children were more likely to rely on sales promotion.

And, the strength of the brand in relation to distributors was
seen as an important influence on the allocation decision. Weaker
brands in this regard were perceived as being likely to require a
greater degree of support from sales promotion activities.

OBSTACLES TO EFFECTIVE
PROMOTIONAL PLANNING

Role of Senior Management

One consistent finding of this study has been the apparent greater
degree of involvement by senior management in the promotional planning process than was found in the earlier study by Robinson and Luck
(1964). This involvement is expressed in several ways: specification
of the total budget for advertising and sales promotion, establishment
of spending guidelines (especially advertising/sales), requirements
for interim and final approvals, and, for almost half the respondents,
classification of brands into groups for different strategic treatments.

The obvious effect of this increased involvement has been to
limit the freedom of the planner, usually the product manager, in the
development of promotional strategies for the brand. In some situations this may be very beneficial. It was found that in some companies
individuals were appointed as product managers with relatively little
experience or spent insufficient time in any one position to develop the
knowledge and experience required to prepare effective programs. In
fact, it appears that much of thc increased involvement by senior management has come about as the result of a recognition that under these
conditions a product manager needed a good deal of guidance.

However, this degree of involvement and control may produce
inflexible strategies, as is perhaps demonstrated in the consistent
pattern of advertising/sales promotion allocations described in Chapter 4. It may also mean that promotional strategy is determined by

individuals who have a less-than-complete knowledge of the brand and its market situation. This can be seen in the target planning stage where budget decisions are likely to be made with only a preliminary review and on the basis of sales projections. These budgets are generally unchanged regardless of the findings of the more comprehensive analysis of the market situation that is undertaken in the strategic planning phase. The overall effect may be to ignore, at least to some extent, the market environment for the brand and to limit a search for optimal strategies. Thus, the brand may meet short-term profit goals, but its long-term position in the market may be seriously impaired (this issue will be discussed later in regard to advertising/ sales promotion strategy). Alternatively, goals may be set too low and prevent the company from realizing the full potential profit from the brand.

It would appear that a more effective approach to the problem of guiding product managers might be to ensure that they receive adequate training and experience before taking over the position. Once they are appointed, they should be encouraged to develop and utilize their understanding of the product and its market by keeping them in that position for longer than the customary year or two. One company that did give its product managers greater responsibility had adopted this approach. The entry-level position was assistant product manager from which the individual was later moved to field sales. After experience in this area, the next appointment was to associate product manager and then, three to five years after joining the company, the individual was promoted to product manager. These positions did not necessarily involve the same product, but the products were usually among a number of closely related items that competed in the same general market category. These individuals thus received a considerable amount of relevant experience and could be given commensurate responsibility.

Ineffective Planning Practices

The first problem area to be considered lies in the objectives that are set for advertising and sales promotion. This study found several instances of failure to set specific objectives—objectives were established but in such a general way that it was impossible to measure whether they were actually achieved. This makes evaluation difficult and may inhibit the development of improved strategies. Another problem was found in the failure to relate objectives to specific promotional tools. There were a number of occasions when promotional objectives were established but with no indication of the role of advertising or sales promotion in achieving those objectives. This

could be the result of unclear thinking, or it could be a failure to recognize the different roles that advertising and sales promotion play in
promotional strategy. Whatever the cause, it serves to further limit
the development of an effective mix of advertising and sales promotion.

One noteworthy exception to both the problems discussed here
was the product manager who developed these objectives for his brand:
to attract X number of new users to the brand, to increase market
share by Y percent, to increase the average frequency of use from
A to B, and to increase distribution to C percent and to reduce out-of
stocks by D percent. The roles of advertising and sales promotion,
then, were made explicit. Advertising was to have the primary role
in achieving the first three objectives with support from sales promotions to attract new users and to encourage more frequent use. Sales
promotion was to be used as the major weapon to increase distribution
and maintain retail stocks.

The setting of the total budget for advertising and sales promotion as a residual from sales after providing for costs and desired
profits may also be an inhibiting factor. It is true that senior management will make some attempt to take the relative position of the
brand into account, but, as noted earlier, this was often based on a
relatively cursory review and may have been undertaken by executives
several levels removed from the marketplace. One effect of this is
that short-term corporate considerations could take precedence over
the long-term health of the brand, which may be converted to a "cash
cow" before its full market potential is achieved.

In regard to the preparation of the plans themselves, the major
problem is the failure to consider alternatives. As was mentioned in
the study, these may be considered informally, but they are not likely
to involve substantive changes. Where alternative plans are not required, then, executives are in danger of developing tunnel vision and
may be unable to look beyond traditional practices for potentially more
effective strategies. The one example of a company that did require
product managers to submit alternative plans was very enlightening.
In this case each product manager was required to submit three plans:
one to maintain market share, one to secure a small increase, and
one to secure a major increase. This forced the product manager to
think about alternatives that included some major changes in the promotional mix and also forced a reconsideration at all levels of the effects of the total advertising and sales promotion budget that had been
set.

In regard to restrictions on the techniques that planners can use,
the companies appeared to be wise in their preference for consumer
promotions rather than sales promotion activities directed to the
trade. The situation described by Weber (1973) indicates the disas-
trous effects on profits when a product manager unleashes a trade

promotion war. Even without a war, the company may receive little for its expenditures. The results of a study by Chevalier and Curhan (1975) showed that in half the cases the trade allowance was simply pocketed by the retail chain with no extra promotional effort on behalf of the brand.

While the role of the functional specialists varied from company to company and according to the individuals involved, it was possible to see some common patterns. The relationship between the product manager and sales management appears to have moved in a more positive direction from that observed in the Robinson and Luck (1964) study. The product managers in this study appeared to be less restricted in this regard than those in the earlier study. On the other hand, the relationship with the advertising and sales promotion executives is still in a state of flux. The net result is that both these specialists appear to be underutilized in the promotional planning process. The advertising specialist virtually disappeared from the planning process with the enthusiastic adoption of the product manager concept. However, several companies are now recognizing the value of having a centralized body of advertising experience and reported that they were trying to make greater use of the advertising specialist to develop more effective advertising programs.

In contrast, the sales promotion specialist position is relatively new. During the interviews there was found to be a wide variation in the experience and qualifications of the executives in this area, but, even in companies where these executives were experienced and highly competent, their skills did not appear to be fully recognized by the product managers. This is reflected in the product managers' view of the sales promotion specialists as resources to draw on as required rather than as experts who should be consulted as a matter of course. Similarly, the extensive experience of outside sales promotion agencies was little utilized in the planning stage. In both these areas there appears to be a great amount to be learned from past experience, and companies that fail to exploit it are condemned to "reinvent the wheel."

The other major area of suboptimization seems to be in the nature of the information that is available to aid the decision maker and the extent to which it is used. The two major problem areas are the lack of information regarding appropriate allocations to advertising and sales promotion and the failure to adequately measure program effectiveness, especially in regard to sales promotion programs. Very few instances were found where there was systematic research into the effects of different promotional mixes. It is reasonable to say that more than 90 percent of the allocation decisions made by executives in the study were made without the benefit of formal research guidance. This does not mean that the promotional mixes were automatically suboptimal, but it does mean that there was no objective information available to test their optimality.

In regard to measuring program effectiveness, there appeared to be little effort either to pretest sales promotion programs or to evaluate them as to their profitability. The failure to pretest programs has important implications because the one company that had conducted an extensive series of tests—using diary panels for several years—reported that there were clear differences in the effectiveness of different sales promotions, depending on their execution. Another company was forced into pretesting some of its sales promotion programs when one proved substantially more expensive than expected.

For both advertising and sales promotion, there was likely to be little attention given to the evaluation of programs in terms of their effectiveness, especially in regard to their profitability. Much sales promotion evaluation appeared to consist of a simple count of the number of cases of the brand that were sold during the promotional period without consideration of the effect on contribution or the slump in sales that usually followed. It is important to monitor impact on profits because any trade allowance or other incentives that are offered come directly from the brand contribution and may have a serious effect. A $1-per-case allowance on a brand with a $2-per-case contribution has to double sales to produce the same total profit.

Allocation Methods

The observed allocation methods could be described as an attempt to avoid the difficulties of optimal decision making through the use of convenient rules of thumb. This appears to be particularly true in the many cases where the planners relied on the allocation that had been established in the preceding year. Unfortunately, there were often no obvious indications that this allocation had been established on anything other than an intuitive basis (although there could have been some adjustments with experience). Such a process can produce considerable circularity in planning: a sales projection based on history leads to a promotional budget based on history, which in turn produces the historical pattern of sales. This, of course, may completely overlook the real potential for the brand.

This pattern also overlooks the fact that different promotional mixes may be more or less appropriate as market conditions change. Buzzell and Farris (1976) have addressed this question in relation to the total advertising and sales promotion budget versus sales-force expenditures and found that there are differences in the appropriate mixes for companies in different market situations. The executives who responded to the survey in this study identified a number of situations where different mixes of advertising and sales promotion were appropriate.

Another weakness in the allocation methods that were used was the perceived failure to exploit the "synergy" inherent in the relationship between advertising and sales promotion. Several studies have found that advertising and sales promotion programs have a greater effect on sales when used together than the same investment would produce if either technique were used on its own (Strang 1975). Two companies had run experiments to test this and were attempting to incorporate the results in their strategies at the time of this study. A third company was reported to have tested various combinations prior to launching a new product and to have adopted the most efficient one. Apart from these companies, there appeared to be little formal recognition of this relationship by the executives who were interviewed.

Promotional Strategies

This study has paid particular attention to the development of advertising and sales promotion strategy—both as it evolves during the planning process and as it is revised after the plans are prepared. One of the principal findings in this area is that executives in many of the companies in the study appeared to be unwilling or unable to understand the relationship between advertising and sales promotion and the role each plays in promotional strategy.

The first evidence of this has already been discussed in relation to the failure to distinguish between advertising and sales promotion in setting promotional objectives. A second indication is the fact that in many cases the strategy is sacrificed to meet short-term objectives. This can be seen in the response to a brand's failure to meet profit objectives—in virtually every case the reaction is to cut back on the budget, especially on advertising. Trade promotion expenditures may be increased a certain amount to compensate. A third example is the perception of a substantial number of survey respondents that it is appropriate to match competitors' advertising/sales promotion strategies, regardless of the market situation.

These actions suggest that many executives in the study may see advertising and sales promotion as substitutes for each other— at least in the short term. But, as anyone familiar with large organizations will recognize, the short term has a habit of becoming the long term, and the allocation histories provided in Chapter 4 indicate that the tendency is for all brands to move toward increased sales promotion and a reduction in advertising. This may have important implications for the long-term profitability of the brand, because there is a small but growing body of evidence that suggests that too great a reliance on sales promotion at the expense of advertising may hasten a brand's decline.

In the market described by Weber (1973), a massive increase in sales promotion expenditures by the three leading brands not only halted their sales growth but also reduced their share of the total market. In a study in the United Kingdom (Television Consumer Audits 1973), it was found that the increased use of price promotions in one market led to a decline in total sales. These and other examples for individual brands are discussed by Strang (1975). There is intuitive support for these findings; by definition a sales promotion device is an additional incentive to attract customers. Customers who are attracted by this device are not likely to make a repeat purchase when the incentive is removed unless they are new to the brand and it offers significant benefits. When these incentives are used frequently, both customers and prospective customers may reasonably be suspicious of the benefits that the brand really does offer. Thus, in the long run a heavily promoted brand is likely to lose sales.

A number of executives recognized this as a possibility but responded to the short-term pressures of the market. This is not necessarily the optimal response, and several "war stories" were reported where a refusal to move from an advertising-oriented strategy or an actual increase in advertising was successful. One of these instances was described by the president of Alberto-Culver (Clarke and Marshall 1973). He noted that in 1972 most shampoo manufacturers were having difficulty with the refusal of retailers to buy in large quantities:

> We could have cut back on advertising, like everyone else in the industry, used lucrative trade deals to get our sales increase, and no one would have noticed. But every company with which we compete was fighting the same inventory-cutting situation. The time seemed right for us to raise the ante.

The company substantially increased its advertising and was rewarded with increased sales. Unfortunately, there is little formal empirically based research on this question.

NEED FOR RESEARCH AND CONCEPTUAL DEVELOPMENT

The field of sales promotion and the relationship between advertising and sales promotion have been largely ignored by many educators and writers in the field of promotional strategy. A 1976 survey of more than 100 four-year colleges found no courses that specifically studied sales promotion. The attitude of many writers is demonstrated by the authors of a recent edition of a widely adopted text in "promotional strategy" when they note that "in addition, under the heading of advertising, is included a variety of incentives for immediate action such as coupons, premiums and price reductions . . . which are sometimes called 'sales promotion'" (Engel, Wales, and Warshaw 1975, p. 5).

It is hoped that the results of this study will encourage the recognition of sales promotion as an important element in promotional strategy. The study of sales promotion is important because of the substantial expenditures in this area and the need for improved management. It needs increased academic attention because marketing students are heavily involved with sales promotion activities in their first or second jobs after graduation.

As a first step in this process, it is clear that there is a great need for a new definition of sales promotion. The present definition is merely a catchall for a wide range of activities that do not fit neatly into the definitions for advertising, personal selling, or publicity. This is scarcely an adequate basis for future research and conceptual development because it includes techniques that operate in completely different ways. Coupons, samples, premiums, and the like offer the prospective customer "something for nothing" (or at least a reduced price); point-of-sales displays and sales brochures draw attention to the product and convey a message in exactly the same way as an advertisement might, while consumer-education programs may have only a tenuous relationship to the sponsoring product or service.

A more appropriate definition might, therefore, view sales promotions as those activities that provide a short-term incentive to encourage purchase or sale of a product or service. This would encompass most of the techniques traditionally associated with sales promotion (sampling, coupons, temporary price reductions, bonus packs, rebates, contests, premiums, trade allowances, and the like) and would provide a common basis for research and conceptual development—namely, the impact of incentives on consumer, trade, or sales-force behavior. This field of study is already well established in the behavioral sciences. The definition would exclude activities such as point-of-sales displays, brochures, cooperative advertising, and others that operate principally as a form of communication similar to advertising.

Beyond the definition stage it is hoped that the findings of this study have contributed to a better understanding of the process by which promotional strategies are actually developed. Among the companies in this study, it would not have been possible to understand the promotional strategy simply by studying the development of the advertising plans and budgets. Promotional strategy was determined as the result of trade-offs among advertising, consumer promotion, and trade-oriented promotion. The process was strongly influenced by senior management and subject to a number of constraints. The final strategy that emerged reflected these factors and many factors in the external environment that this study identified and evaluated.

A FINAL COMMENT

Promotional strategy, in general, and the development of appropriate advertising/sales promotion mixes, in particular, are large and complex issues. They involve a multiplicity of factors both within the organization and in the environment in which they operate. In most cases the impacts of these factors are difficult to assess—they are qualitative rather than quantitative, and they change among individuals and organizations and over time.

Despite the difficulties, these areas are important for future study. There is no doubt that a significant and apparently permanent change has taken place in the relationship between advertising and sales promotion. In part this is a voluntary change; in part this change may be forced by external developments such as the growing power of the retailer in the channel of distribution. Whatever the reason, relatively little is known about the change and its implications.

This study has attempted to improve our understanding of the change and to identify some of the potential implications. Of necessity it is descriptive rather than prescriptive, and it raises more questions than it answers. It is hoped that the findings discussed here will provide a foundation upon which later work can build.

APPENDIX A:
Marketing Science Institute
Advertising/Sales
Promotion Planning Study

MARKETING SCIENCE INSTITUTE

ADVERTISING/SALES PROMOTION PLANNING STUDY

The purpose of this study is to improve our understanding of the way companies manage their advertising and sales promotion activities. There has been relatively little research in this area, especially regarding the increasingly important field of sales promotion, and your experiences will provide valuable insights.

Please take a few moments to answer the following questions relating to: 1) organization structure and responsibilities, 2) the planning and budgeting process, and 3) the evaluation procedures used by your company or division. Please answer the questions as they reflect the *usual procedures* for planning and budgeting for *established* brands (i.e., brands which have been on the market for one year or more) in the division or company where you have major responsibility.

1. Organization Structure

1.1 Which of these best describes your organization? (Please check one)

a. Single Corporate Entity ☐ (06-1)

b. Multidivision Corporation with marketing
staff at both corporate and division levels ☐ (06-2)

c. Multidivision Corporation with marketing
staff only at division levels ☐ (06-3)

d. Other (please describe) ☐ (06-4)

_____

_____

1.2 Does your division or company use the product or brand manager system?
Yes ☐ (07-1) No ☐ (07-2) (If NO please go to Question 1.5)

1.3 (If YES) What is the title of the executive to whom the product/brand managers report? (Please check one)

Marketing Manager ☐ (08-1)	Advertising Manager	☐ (08-3)
Product Group Manager ☐ (08-2)	Other (please give title) _____	☐ (08-4)

1.4 In your organization what is the average number of assistants reporting to a product or brand manager? _____ (Number) (09)

1.5 Does your organization have an executive or executives with specialist responsibilities for advertising and/or sales promotion activities (e.g., Advertising Manager/Director/Vice President)? If yes, please give the specialist's title, the title of the executive to whom the specialist reports, and the approximate time when the specialist position was established.

A. At Corporate Level

Title of Corporate Specialist Responsible for:

		Present Position Established		
		Before 1960	1960-1970	Since 1970
a. Advertising _____	Reports to: _____	☐ (10-1)	☐ (10-2)	☐ (10-3)
b. Sales Promotion _____	Reports to: _____	☐ (11-1)	☐ (11-2)	☐ (11-3)
c. Both Advtg. and S.P. _____	Reports to: _____	☐ (12-1)	☐ (12-2)	☐ (12-3)
d. No such specialist position at corporate level ☐ (13-1)				

B. At Division Level

Title of Division Specialist Responsible for:

		Present Position Established		
		Before 1960	1960-1970	Since 1970
a. Advertising _____	Reports to: _____	☐ (14-1)	☐ (14-2)	☐ (14-3)
b. Sales Promotion _____	Reports to: _____	☐ (15-1)	☐ (15-2)	☐ (15-3)
c. Both Advtg. and S.P. _____	Reports to: _____	☐ (16-1)	☐ (16-2)	☐ (16-3)
d. No such specialist position at division level ☐ (17-1)				

Marketing Science Institute is a non-profit research center in the field of marketing, associated with the Harvard Business School, and principally supported by business.

1.6 **Your title:** _____ (18)

1.7 On the following list of <u>advertising-related</u> activities please indicate the extent to which the advertising (or advertising and sales promotion) specialist and staff are involved. (Circle appropriate number.) Please respond for division and corporate specialists as appropriate.

	Division Specialist			Corporate Specialist			
Advertising Activity	*Not Involved*	*Consulted*	*Responsible*	*Not Involved*	*Consulted*	*Responsible*	
Advertising Research	1	2	3	1	2	3	(19-20)
Selection of Advertising Agency	1	2	3	1	2	3	(21-22)
Media Planning	1	2	3	1	2	3	(23-24)
Media Buying	1	2	3	1	2	3	(25-26)
Brand Copy Creation	1	2	3	1	2	3	(27-28)
Brand Copy Approval	1	2	3	1	2	3	(29-30)
Legal Clearance of Advertising	1	2	3	1	2	3	(31-32)
Corporate Advertising Preparation	1	2	3	1	2	3	(33-34)
Coordination of Multiproduct Advertising Campaigns	1	2	3	1	2	3	(35-36)
Brand Advertising Budgets	1	2	3	1	2	3	(37-38)
Other Advertising Activities	1	2	3	1	2	3	(39-40)

(specify) _____

_____

1.8 What is the size of the specialist staff that is responsible for the <u>advertising-related</u> activities described above?

a. At division level? _____ (41)

b. At the corporate level? _____ (42)

1.9 For the following list of <u>sales promotion-related</u> activities, please indicate the extent to which the sales promotion (or advertising and sales promotion) specialist and staff are involved. (Circle appropriate number.) Please respond for division and corporate specialists as appropriate.

	Division Specialist			Corporate Specialist			
Sales Promotion Activity	*Not Involved*	*Consulted*	*Responsible*	*Not Involved*	*Consulted*	*Responsible*	
Sales Promotion Research	1	2	3	1	2	3	(43-44)
Selection of Sales Promotion Agency	1	2	3	1	2	3	(45-46)
Design of Consumer Sales Promotion Materials (including point of sale)	1	2	3	1	2	3	(47-48)
Approve Sales Promotion Materials	1	2	3	1	2	3	(49-50)
Design Sales Literature	1	2	3	1	2	3	(51-52)
Plan Sales Meetings	1	2	3	1	2	3	(53-54)
Trade Show Participation	1	2	3	1	2	3	(55-56)
Coordination Multiproduct Sales Promotion Campaigns	1	2	3	1	2	3	(57-58)
Brand Consumer Promotion Budgets	1	2	3	1	2	3	(59-60)
Brand Trade Promotion Budgets	1	2	3	1	2	3	(61-62)
Other Sales Promotion Activities	1	2	3	1	2	3	(63-64)

(specify) _____

_____

1.10 What is the size of the specialist staff that is responsible for the <u>sales promotion-related</u> activities described above?

a. At division level? _____ (65)

b. At the corporate level? _____ (66)

112

2. Planning and Budgeting

2.1 Which of the following marketing planning activities are primarily the responsibility of:

- The product or brand manager (check appropriate box in first column).
- Another executive or committee within the company (please give title of executive or name of committee).
- An outside organization (please indicate kind of firm, e.g., advertising agency).

If the activity is not undertaken at all, please check the appropriate box in the last column.

Activity	Product Manager	Another Executive or Committee (title/name) or Outside Organization (kind)	Not Undertaken	
Establish Sales Targets for Brand	☐ 2	_____	☐ 1	(67)
Set Other Marketing Goals for Brand	☐ 2	_____	☐ 1	(68)
Evaluate Market Situation for Brand	☐ 2	_____	☐ 1	(69)
Establish Objectives for Brand Advertising	☐ 2	_____	☐ 1	(70)
Establish Objectives for Brand Sales Promotion	☐ 2	_____	☐ 1	(71)
Prepare Brand Advertising Program	☐ 2	_____	☐ 1	(72)
Prepare Brand Consumer Promotion Program	☐ 2	_____	☐ 1	(73)
Prepare Brand Trade Promotion Program	☐ 2	_____	☐ 1	(74)
Prepare Complete Brand Marketing Plan	☐ 2	_____	☐ 1	(75)
Final Approval of Brand Marketing Plan	☐ 2	_____	☐ 1	(76)

2.2 Which of the following marketing budgeting activities are primarily the responsibility of:
- The product or brand manager (check appropriate box in first column).
- Another executive or committee within the company (please give title of executive or name of committee).
- An outside organization (please indicate kind of firm, e.g., advertising agency).

If the activity is not undertaken at all, please check the appropriate box in the last column.

Activity	Product Manager	Another Executive or Committee (title/name) or Outside Organization (kind)	Not Undertaken	
Establish Financial Goals for Brand	☐ 2	_____	☐ 1	(06)
Establish the Preliminary Marketing Budget for Brand	☐ 2	_____	☐ 1	(07)
Establish the Preliminary Advertising Budget for Brand	☐ 2	_____	☐ 1	(08)
Establish the Preliminary Sales Promotion Budget for Brand	☐ 2	_____	☐ 1	(09)
Prepare Detailed Advertising Budget	☐ 2	_____	☐ 1	(10)
Prepare Detailed Consumer Promotion Budget	☐ 2	_____	☐ 1	(11)
Prepare Detailed Trade Promotion Budget	☐ 2	_____	☐ 1	(12)
Approve Advertising Budget	☐ 2	_____	☐ 1	(13)
Approve Consumer Promotion Budget	☐ 2	_____	☐ 1	(14)
Approve Trade Promotion Budget	☐ 2	_____	☐ 1	(15)

2.3 This question focuses on organizational units rather than on functions as above. Various organizational units are often involved in the planning and budgeting process for advertising and sales promotion. For each of the following departments, indicate the role of their personnel in advertising and/or sales promotion planning and budgeting for established brands in your division or company. (Please circle the appropriate number.)

Department	No Such Department In Organization	Role in Advertising Planning				Role in Sales Promotion Planning				
		Not Involved	Consulted	Prepares Proposals or Guides	Approves	Involved	Consulted	Prepares Proposals or Guides	Approves	
Corporate Planning	5	1	2	3	4	1	2	3	4	(16-17)
Marketing Research	5	1	2	3	4	1	2	3	4	(18-19)
Sales Management	5	1	2	3	4	1	2	3	4	(20-21)
Corporate Finance	5	1	2	3	4	1	2	3	4	(22-23)
Division Finance	5	1	2	3	4	1	2	3	4	(24-25)
Corporate Marketing	5	1	2	3	4	1	2	3	4	(26-27)
Corporate Advertising	5	1	2	3	4	1	2	3	4	(28-29)
Corporate Sales Promotion	5	1	2	3	4	1	2	3	4	(30-31)
Division Marketing	5	1	2	3	4	1	2	3	4	(32-33)
Division Advertising	5	1	2	3	4	1	2	3	4	(34-35)
Division Sales Promotion	5	1	2	3	4	1	2	3	4	(36-37)
Advertising Agency	5	1	2	3	4	1	2	3	4	(38-39)
Sales Promotion Agency	5	1	2	3	4	1	2	3	4	(40-41)
Other Units with Major Involvement (specify):		1	2	3	4	1	2	3	4	(42-43)

_____

2.4 The following questions relate to factors which influence the allocation of funds to advertising or sales promotion and to changes in budgets during the fiscal year.

A. In which of the following areas are guidelines or recommendations made by senior executives regarding the allocation of funds to advertising or sales promotion for established brands? (Please check each item where such guidelines are made.)

Total dollar amount for advertising sales
  and promotion □ (42-1)
Percentage of advertising to sales □ (43-1)
Percentage of sales promotion to sales □ (44-1)
Percentage of advertising to sales
  promotion □ (45-1)
Classification of brands into strategic
  clusters for different strategic treatment □ (46-1)
Other areas of senior executives' guide-
  lines or recommendations (specify): □ (47-1)

_____

_____

B. In the course of the past fiscal year, roughly how many changes of 10% or more would have been made in budgeted advertising or sales promotion expenditures for established brands? (If there were no changes, please go to Question 2.5.)

	Advertising	Sales Promotion
a. None	□ (48-1)	□ (49-1)
b. One or two	□ (48-2)	□ (49-2)
c. Three or more	□ (48-3)	□ (49-3)

C. Approximately what proportion of these changes would be initiated by senior division or corporate executives?

	Corporation	Division
a. Practically none	□ (50-1)	□ (51-1)
b. Less than half	□ (50-2)	□ (51-2)
c. About half	□ (50-3)	□ (51-3)
d. More than half	□ (50-4)	□ (51-4)
e. Practically all	□ (50-5)	□ (51-5)

D. In which directions did these changes affect budgeted expenditures? (Please answer for each item.)

	Increase	Decrease	Both Directions During Year
Total Advertising and Sales Promotion budget	☐ (52-1)	☐ (52-2)	☐ (52-3)
Advertising budget	☐ (53-1)	☐ (53-2)	☐ (53-3)
Consumer promotion budget	☐ (54-1)	☐ (54-2)	☐ (54-3)
Trade promotion budget	☐ (55-1)	☐ (55-2)	☐ (55-3)

E. What were the two or three most common reasons for these changes?

_____

_____

_____
(56-57)

2.5 Some characteristics of an established brand may tend to increase the importance of advertising relative to sales promotion; other characteristics may tend to increase the importance of sales promotion relative to advertising. In your judgment which of the following factors do you think would tend to increase the importance of advertising over sales promotion, increase the importance of sales promotion over advertising, or have neither effect on expenditures? (Please circle the appropriate number.)

	Increase Advertising Over Sales Promotion	Increase Sales Promotion Over Advertising	Neither Effect	
Brand has a contribution rate above *division* average	1	2	3	(58)
Brand has a contribution rate above *corporate* average	1	2	3	(59)
Brand has the largest share of any brand in its market	1	2	3	(60)
Brand has one or more competitors with similar market shares	1	2	3	(61)
Brand is at introductory stage of life cycle	1	2	3	(62)
Brand is at growth stage of life cycle	1	2	3	(63)
Brand is at mature stage of life cycle	1	2	3	(64)
Brand is at decline stage of life cycle	1	2	3	(65)
Brand is facing a major competing brand which has just cut advertising and increased sales promotion expenditures	1	2	3	(66)
Brand is facing major competing brand which has just increased advertising and cut sales promotion expenditures	1	2	3	(67)
Brand is in a market where private labels have more than 25% of total sales volume	1	2	3	(68)
Brand is sold only in limited geographical regions or markets	1	2	3	(69)
Brand has a highly seasonal sales pattern (more than 40% of sales in one quarter)	1	2	3	(70)
Brand is purchased by consumers typically once every month or more frequently	1	2	3	(71)
Brand is considered to be well differentiated from competing national brands	1	2	3	(72)
Brand sells at a higher price than competing national brands	1	2	3	(73)
Consumers report the brand to be of higher quality than competing national brands	1	2	3	(74)
Brand is in danger of losing national distribution	1	2	3	(75)
Brand is not meeting sales targets	1	2	3	(76)
Brand is not meeting profit targets	1	2	3	(77)
Brand is ahead of sales targets	1	2	3	(78)
Brand is in a product category that is ahead of profit targets	1	2	3	(79)

2.6 Are there any other factors which you think might cause . . .

a. Advertising to be more important than sales promotion?

_____

_____

_____

(06)

b. Sales promotion to be more important than advertising?

_____

_____

_____

(07)

3. Research and Evaluation of Advertising and Sales Promotion

3.1 Which of these measures, if any, are normally used to evaluate advertising and sales promotion programs for major established brands in your division or company? Check all boxes that apply.

	Advertising	Sales Promotion	
	(08-09)	(10-11)	
No formal evaluation	☐	☐	(01)
Consumer awareness measures	☐	☐	(02)
Consumer attitude measures	☐	☐	(03)
Consumer panel data	☐	☐	(04)
Sales volume (units)	☐	☐	(05)
Sales volume ($)	☐	☐	(06)
Share of market	☐	☐	(07)
Distribution level	☐	☐	(08)
Profitability	☐	☐	(09)
Executive judgment	☐	☐	(10)
Other (specify):	☐	☐	(11)

_____

_____

3.2 In the aggregate, about what percentage of sales for established brands would be budgeted for research in advertising and sales promotion?

	Advertising	Sales Promotion	
	(12)	(13)	
a. None	☐	☐	(1)
b. Less than ¼ of 1%	☐	☐	(2)
c. Between ¼ of 1% and 1%	☐	☐	(3)
d. More than 1%	☐	☐	(4)
e. Not applicable for our company or division	☐	☐	(5)

116

3.3 Are formal quantitative models used to aid advertising and/or sales promotion decision-making? (Please check all appropriate applications.)

	Advertising	Sales Promotion
	(15)	(16)
No quantitative models used	☐	☐ (1)
Models used for allocating total funds to advertising and sales promotion	☐	☐ (2)
Models used for allocating funds to advertising	☐	☐ (3)
Models used for allocating funds to sales promotion	☐	☐ (4)
Models used for media planning and selection	☐	☐ (5)
Other (specify): _____	☐	☐ (6)

4. Classification Questions

4.1 Which of the following categories was the largest single source of sales for your division or company in fiscal 1975?

- a. Dry groceries ☐ (16-1)
- b. Perishables (meat, frozen food, fruit, vegetables) ☐ (16-2)
- c. Beer, wine, or liquor ☐ (16-3)
- d. Other beverages (e.g., soft drinks, coffee) ☐ (16-4)
- e. Personal care/toiletries ☐ (16-5)
- f. Household non-food products ☐ (16-6)
- g. Other (specify): _____ ☐ (16-7)

4.2 What were the approximate sales of your division or company in fiscal 1975?

- a. Less than $1 million ☐ (17-1)
- b. $1-9 million ☐ (17-2)
- c. $10-24 million ☐ (17-3)
- d. $25-49 million ☐ (17-4)
- e. $50-99 million ☐ (17-5)
- f. $100 million or more ☐ (17-6)

4.3 Relative to the amount spent by your division or company on media advertising, would you say that the amount spent on sales promotion (including consumer and trade promotion) was:

- a. Significantly more than on advertising ☐ (18-1)
- b. Somewhat more than on advertising ☐ (18-2)
- c. Roughly the same as on advertising ☐ (18-3)
- d. Somewhat less than on advertising ☐ (18-4)
- e. Significantly less than on advertising ☐ (18-5)

4.4 If your company or division is part of a larger corporation, which category was the largest single source of sales for the corporation in fiscal 1975?

- a. Consumer durable goods ☐ (19-1)
- b. Consumer non-durable goods ☐ (19-2)
- c. Industrial goods ☐ (19-3)
- d. Consumer services ☐ (19-4)
- e. Other (specify): _____ ☐ (19-5)

4.5 If your company or division is part of a larger corporation, what were the approximate total sales of the corporation in fiscal 1975?

- a. Less than $10 million ☐ (20-1)
- b. $10-49 million ☐ (20-2)
- c. $50-99 million ☐ (20-3)
- d. $100-499 million ☐ (20-4)
- e. $500 million or more ☐ (20-5)

Are there any general comments about advertising and promotion which you would like to add — or any suggestions for questions not included in the questionnaire?

_____

_____

_____

_____

_____

_____

_____

5. Telephone Interview and Reporting of Results

5.1 In conjunction with this study we are contacting a small number of executives for a brief telephone conversation to seek additional perspectives on these areas. If you are willing to speak further on the considerations involved in planning and allocating advertising and sales promotion expenditures for product marketing, please circle "yes" and indicate your name, company, and phone number in Question 5.2.

                    Yes   No

5.2 Your name and company (optional)

Name _____

Company _____

Address _____

_____

Phone No. _____

5.3 If you would like a summary of the results of the study, please write your name above, or, if you prefer to maintain anonymity for this questionnaire, drop us a separate note on your letterhead with a request for results.

If the return envelope has been separated from this
questionnaire, please send the completed
questionnaire to:

Advertising/Promotion Study
MARKETING SCIENCE INSTITUTE
14 Story Street
Cambridge, Massachusetts 02138

THANK YOU VERY MUCH

APPENDIX B:
Interview Guide for Field Visits

Background

    Organizational structure

    Marketing planning procedure

    Marketing budgeting procedure

Corporate/Division Policies

    Advertising practices

    Sales promotion practices

    General research studies and other information

    Conclusions

Clinical Example

    Product/brand history

    Planning and budgeting procedure

    Advertising and sales promotion decisions

    Research studies

    Conclusions

Industry

    History

    Changes in advertising and sales promotion

    Predictions

    Comments

APPENDIX C:

Screening Procedure for
Advertising Age/ANA Sample Responses

The basic procedure was to begin with the responses from the Advertising Age sample and add responses from the Association of National Advertisers (ANA) list as they satisfied various tests against the possibility of overlap. (The questionnaires were of different colors.) These tests are described below, together with the respondent numbers of the questionnaires that were added.

1. All respondents from the Advertising Age sample reported multidivision organization with decentralized marketing except one (Quaker Oats number 0155). This response was compared with similar companies on the ANA list and numbers 106, 109, 114, 119, 122, 133, and 139 were found to be different.

2. A comparison of all responses from multidivision companies with marketing at both levels found no duplicates so included numbers 101, 107, 110, 113, 115, 116, 125, 127, 131, and 137.

3. Only one respondent on the Advertising Age list did not use the product manager system, and individual comparison with similar companies on the ANA list showed no duplicates so included numbers 111, 126, and 138.

4. No product manager in an Advertising Age company had more than two assistants so included numbers 108, 123, 128, and 130, where a greater number of assistants was reported.

5. Only one Advertising Age company reported that their major corporate business was in durables, industrial goods, or services so compared with similar ANA businesses and included numbers 100, 102, 112, 135, 136, and 141.

6. Only three Advertising Age respondents had corporate sales of $100 million to $499 million so compared with ANA and included numbers 104 and 140.

7. A comparison of the number and location of advertising and sales promotion specialists allowed the inclusion of numbers 105, 120, 124, and 134.

Sample or List	Number
ANA	
Total responses	42
Duplication	1
Reject for insufficient data	1
Industrial company	4
Net number used	36

Sample or List	Number
Advertising Age	
Total responses	22
Duplication	1
Net number used	21
Total usable responses	57

TABLE C.1

Comparison of Samples

Parameter	Total Number	Advertising Age	ANA
Organization			
Single corporate entity	7	0	7
Multidivision corporation			
Marketing staff at both levels	11	1	10
Marketing staff at division levels only	39	20	19
Products sold			
Dry groceries	18	8	10
Perishables	4	1	3
Personal care/toiletries	16	9	7
Household nonfood	19	3	13
Size of division sales			
(millions of dollars)			
Less than 100	1	0	1
100 to 499	10	3	7
500 or greater	39	18	21
Not available	7	0	7

Source: Compiled by the author.

121

BIBLIOGRAPHY

"Advertising, Marketing Reports on the 100 Top National Advertis-
    ers." 1976. Advertising Age 47 (August 23): 27-166.

American Marketing Association. 1960. "Marketing Definitions: A
    Glossary of Marketing Terms." Chicago.

Ames, B. Charles. 1968. "Marketing Planning for Industrial Prod-
    ucts." Harvard Business Review, vol. 46, no. 5 (September-
    October).

Assael, Henry. 1976. "Segmenting Markets by Response Elasticity."
    Journal of Marketing Research 16 (April): 27-35.

Axiom Market Research Bureau. 1974. "1974 Target Group Index
    Survey." New York.

Banks, Seymour. 1973. "Trends Affecting the Implementation of
    Advertising and Promotion." Journal of Marketing, vol. 47,
    no. 1 (January).

Bauer, Raymond A. 1972. "Notes on a Strategy of Research on
    Complex Organizational Processes." Mimeographed. Boston:
    Harvard Business School.

Booz, Allen & Hamilton. 1974. 1973 Study of Grocery Trade Deal-
    ing. New York: Booz, Allen & Hamilton.

Borden, Neil H. 1964. "The Concept of the Marketing Mix." Jour-
    nal of Advertising Research 4 (June): 2-7.

Boston Consulting Group. 1970. "The Product Portfolio." Perspec-
    tives. Boston: BCG.

Bowman, R. D. 1974. "Merchandising and Promotion Grow Big in
    Marketing World." Advertising Age, vol. 45, no. 52 (Decem-
    ber 30).

Boyd, Harper W., Jr., and William F. Massey. 1972. Marketing
    Management. New York: Harcourt Brace Jovanovich.

Buell, Victor P. 1975. "The Changing Role of the Product Manager." Journal of Marketing 39 (July): 3-11.

_____. 1973. "Changing Practices in Advertising Decision-Making and Control." Mimeographed. New York: Association of National Advertisers.

Buzzell, R. D., and Paul W. Farris. 1976. "Marketing Costs in Selected Consumer Goods Industries." Working Paper no. 76-111, Marketing Science Institute, Cambridge, Mass.

Buzzell, R. D., Bradley T. Gale, and Ralph G. M. Sultan. 1974. "Market Share, Profitability, and Business Strategy." Working Paper, Marketing Science Institute, Cambridge, Mass. Mimeographed.

Buzzell, R. D., et al. 1972. Marketing: A Contemporary Analysis. 2d ed. New York: McGraw-Hill.

Campbell, Roy H. 1969. Measuring the Sales and Profit Results of Advertising. New York: Association of National Advertisers.

Chevalier, Michel. 1975. "Increase in Sales due to In-Store Display." Journal of Marketing Research 12 (November): 426-31.

Chevalier, M., and R. Curhan. 1975. "Temporary Promotions as a Function of Trade Deals." Working Paper, Marketing Science Institute, Cambridge, Mass. Mimeographed.

Christopher, M. 1972a. Marketing Below the Line. London: George Allen & Unwin.

_____. 1972b. "Researching below the Line," Admap (January).

Clarke, Roberta N., and Martin V. Marshall. 1973. "Alberto-Culver Company: Calm 2." ICCH no. 9-573-069, Boston.

Clewett, R. M., and S. F. Stasch. 1975. "Shifting Role of the Product Manager." Harvard Business Review 53 (January-February): 91-96.

Courtney, Alice E. 1970. "Practitioner's Conceptions of the Advertising Process: An Initial Look." Working Paper, Marketing Science Institute, Cambridge, Mass. Mimeographed.

Davis, Nancy J., and Benson P. Shapiro. 1974. "Vick Chemical Company, Incorporated." ICCH no. 2-575-005, Boston. Mimeographed.

Engel, J. F., H. G. Wales, and M. R. Warshaw. 1975. Promotional Strategy. 3d ed. Homewood, Ill.: Richard D. Irwin.

Hopkins, David S. 1972. The Short-Term Marketing Plan. New York: National Industrial Conference Board.

Hurwood, D. L. 1968. Advertising, Sales Promotion and Public Relations—Organizational Alternatives. New York: National Industrial Conference Board.

Kotler, Philip A. 1972. Marketing Management: Analysis Planning and Control. 2d ed. Englewood Cliffs, N.J.: Prentice-Hall.

_____. 1971. Marketing Decision Making: A Model Building Approach. New York: Holt, Rinehart and Winston.

Lucas, D. B. 1972. "Point of View: Product Managers in Advertising." Journal of Advertising Research 12: 41-44.

March, James G., and Herbert A. Simon. 1958. Organizations. New York: John Wiley & Sons.

Marschner, Donald C. 1967. "Theory versus Practice in Allocating Advertising Money." Journal of Business, July, pp. 286-302.

Marshall, Martin V. 1975. "Regular Maxwell House Coffee." Rev. ed. ICCH no. 9-569-001, Boston. Mimeographed.

Nielsen Company, A. C. 1976. Nielsen Researcher, no. 4. Northbrook, Ill.

Peckham, J. O., Sr. 1973. The Wheel of Marketing. Chicago: A. C. Nielsen.

Permut, S. E., A. J. Michel, and M. Joseph. 1977. "How European Managers Set Advertising Budgets." Journal of Advertising Research, no. 17 (October), pp. 75-79.

_____. 1976. "The Researchers Sample: A Review of Choice of Respondent in Marketing Research." Journal of Marketing Research 13 (August): 278-83.

Robinson, P. J., and D. J. Luck. 1964. Promotional Decision Making: Practice and Theory. New York: McGraw-Hill.

Robinson, P. J., et al. 1967. Promotional Decisions Using Mathematical Models. Boston: Allyn and Bacon.

Ryan, John G., and James D. Scott. 1977. "Pfizer, Inc., Leeming/ Pacquin Division (A)." In Introduction to Marketing Management by Steward H. Rewoldt, et al., 3d ed. Homewood, Ill.: Irwin.

San Augustine, A. J., and W. F. Foley. 1975. "How Large Advertisers Set Budgets." Journal of Advertising Research 15 (October): 11-16.

Singer, Harvey N., and Stewart F. DeBruicker. 1975a. "General Foods Corporation: Tang Instant Breakfast Drink." Rev. ed. ICCH no. 2-575-063, Boston. Mimeographed.

_____. 1975b. "L'eggs Products, Inc (A)." ICCH no. 9-575-065, Boston. Mimeographed.

Spratlen, Thaddeus H. 1962. "An Appraisal of Theory and Practice in the Allocation of Sales Effort." Ph.D. dissertation, Ohio State University, Columbus, Ohio.

Strang, Roger A. 1975. The Relationship between Advertising and Promotion in Brand Strategy. Cambridge, Mass: Marketing Science Institute.

Sunoo, D., and L. Y. S. Lin. 1978. "Sales Effects of Promotion and Advertising." Journal of Advertising Research 18 (October): 37-40.

Television Consumer Audits. 1973. "The Quantification of Below the Line Expenditure." Spotlight on Marketing, vol. 2, no. 3 (May/ June).

Udell, Jon G. 1968. "The Perceived Importance of the Elements of Strategy." Journal of Marketing 32 (January): 34-40.

Weber, R. J. 1973. "How Trade Allowances Are Making Mincemeat Out of Project Objectives." Association of National Advertisers Financial Management Workshop, Montauk, N.Y., June.

Winkler, John. 1972. Winkler on Marketing Planning. New York: John Wiley & Sons.

INDEX

ABOUT THE AUTHOR

ROGER STRANG is Assistant Professor of Marketing in the Graduate School of Business Administration at the University of Southern California. A New Zealander, he graduated from the University of Otago and worked in marketing for a leading food manufacturer for three years. He completed his M.B.A. at Michigan State University and his D.B.A. at Harvard University. He has taught at the University of Otago and has been a member of the research staff at the Marketing Science Institute, Cambridge, Massachusetts.

Dr. Strang's other publications include The Relationship between Advertising and Promotion in Brand Strategy (Marketing Science Institute) and the forthcoming Sales Promotion Research: The State of the Art (Association of National Advertisers).